高职进阶

实用英语口语

College Practical Oral English

主　编：刘　爽　刘亚丽

副主编：杨晓宇　郑　颖　李彩云

山东人民出版社·济南

国家一级出版社　全国百佳图书出版单位

图书在版编目（CIP）数据

高职进阶：实用英语口语 / 刘爽，刘亚丽主编 .— 济南：山东人民出版社，2024.1（2025.1重印）

ISBN 978-7-209-14880-1

Ⅰ. ①高… Ⅱ. ①刘… ②刘… Ⅲ. ①英语－口语－高等职业教育－教材 Ⅳ. ①H319.32

中国国家版本馆CIP数据核字（2023）第232830号

高职进阶：实用英语口语

GAOZHI JINJIE: SHIYONG YINGYU KOUYU

刘　爽　刘亚丽　主编

主管单位　山东出版传媒股份有限公司
出版发行　山东人民出版社
出 版 人　胡长青
社　　址　济南市市中区舜耕路517号
邮　　编　250003
电　　话　总编室（0531）82098914
　　　　　市场部（0531）82098965
网　　址　http://www.sd-book.com.cn
印　　装　济南新先锋彩印有限公司
经　　销　新华书店

规　　格　16开（184mm × 260mm）
印　　张　17.25
字　　数　230千字
版　　次　2024年1月第1版
印　　次　2025年1月第2次
ISBN 978-7-209-14880-1
定　　价　52.00元

编委会

主　　编　刘　爽（济南职业学院）

　　　　　刘亚丽（济南职业学院）

副 主 编　杨晓宇（济南职业学院）

　　　　　郑　颖（济南职业学院）

　　　　　李彩云（济南职业学院）

参　　编　刘晓璐（济南职业学院）

　　　　　饶　萌（济南职业学院）

　　　　　严拥庆（山东天天书房教育科技有限公司）

　　　　　赵晓栋（山东天天书房教育科技有限公司）

　　　　　贾　凤（济南职业学院）

　　　　　孙建春（济南职业学院）

　　　　　郭超来（济南职业学院）

　　　　　杨爱军（济南职业学院）

　　　　　张　莹（济南职业学院）

　　　　　王　乐（济南职业学院）

　　　　　陈瑞彩（济南职业学院）

　　　　　刘　君（济南职业学院）

　　　　　毛雪娇（济南职业学院）

前　言

新时期，国家和社会对高等教育提出了更高的要求，即大力培养掌握党和国家方针政策、具有全球视野、通晓国际规则、熟练运用外语、精通中外谈判和沟通的国际化人才，以及有针对性地培养能够推动“一带一路”高质量发展的各类专业技术和管理人才。在此背景下，高职英语教学应适应我国高等教育，尤其是高等职业教育发展的新形势，充分发挥英语语言的工具性、人文性和国际性，满足新时期国家和社会对高素质技术技能人才的需求，切实提高学生的英语交际能力。

《高职进阶：实用英语口语》的编写依据《高等职业教育专科英语课程标准（2021年版）》，以职业需求为导向、以实践能力培养为重点，有机融入课程思政理念，全面落实立德树人的根本任务，体现了高职英语教学的职业性、实践性、人文性和国际性。教材按照学生从校园到职场的真实情境进行设计，共15个单元，每单元围绕一个生活或学习情境展开，涵盖了高职英语口语从语音到词汇再到情境表达的多层次能力要求。本教材旨在训练学生在校园和职场环境中的英语口语表达能力，在职业情境中准确使用英语进行交际的能力，以及团队合作等职业素养。

本教材的编写理念为：以立德树人为根本任务，以新课程标准为引领，以生活和职业情境为主线，以培养学生英语学科核心素养为目标。教材内容紧扣时代发展主题，兼具知识性和趣味性，有助于引导学生自主学习语言知识，训练语言技能，提升语言思维，其最终目的是培养学生成为具有中国情怀、国际视野，能够在日常生活和职场中用英语进行有效沟通的高素质技术技能人才。

本教材具有以下特色：

1.校企合作，协同开发。山东天天书房教育科技有限公司深度参与本教材的编写，针对岗位需求，提出学生学习英语口语具体可行的标准。据此，校企双方共同设计了真实的职场情境，使用来自企业一线的真实语料，直接训练学生在未来职场所需技能，培养学生的职业核心素养。

2.情境化编写体例，学练兼顾。全书以两名高职学生的校园与职场实践为主线，模拟高职学生从入学到就业的全过程，全书设计15个情境，在每一情境中围绕同一主题进行循序渐进的口语训练，兼顾语料输入与语言输出，不仅能够有效引导学习者学习相关知识，而且有助于提升其口语技能。各情境编写框架如下：

Learning Objectives 学习目标
↓
Topic Words and Expressions 主题词汇
↓
Lead-in 情境引入
↓
Dialogs 情境对话
↓
Passage 情境语篇
↓
Exercises 口语训练
↓
Self-evaluation 自我评价
↓
Culture 文化拓展

3.教材内容对接行业与职场，服务于职业素养训练。编写教师均有长期的行业企业实践经历，具备双师资格。教材紧密贴合高职学生校园生活和未来职业，通过丰富多样的练习，鼓励学生积极参与、大胆创新。多种形式的小组合作任务，要求学生开展合作学习，提升其表达能力和团队合作意识。

4.立体化资源丰富，便于移动终端学习。教材配有PPT课件、音频、视频，均以二维码形式呈现，学习者扫码即可学习。丰富多样的资源，立体新颖的方式使学生可以即学即练。

5.有效融入课程思政，引导学生树立正确的世界观、人生观和价值观。教材内容有机融入社会主义核心价值观、中华优秀传统文化，涉及中华饮食、传统节庆、移动支付、现代农业、航空航天、终身学习等方面，以多种形式展现了中国的特色风貌和新时代职业精神。以上思政元素的融入，不仅有助于学生学习语言，更有利于其提升认知能力与思想水平。

本教材的使用范围较广，既可作为高等职业院校的英语口语教材使用，也适合有志于提升英语口语能力的社会人员自学使用。

本书由刘爽、刘亚丽统筹策划，由刘爽、刘亚丽、杨晓宇、郑颖、李彩云以及来自山东天天书房教育科技有限公司的严拥庆、赵晓栋共同编写，视频资源由刘爽、刘亚丽、杨晓宇制作。同时，感谢各位参编老师的大力支持。由于编者水平有限，书中难免有不妥之处，敬请广大读者批评指正。

编　者

2024年1月

CONTENTS

Unit 1

Campus Life

扫码看

Learning Objectives

After learning this unit, you should be able to:

1. get familiar with the words and expressions concerning campus life;
2. talk about your daily life on campus;
3. get accustomed to college life and know how to be a student with the spirit of the new era.

Unit 1

Part 1 Topic Words and Expressions

扫码听

The Student Society

- notice board
- society
- poster
- recruit
- prefer
- stretch
- advanced
- applicant
- regret
- potential
- Chances are slim.

Borrowing and Returning Books

- self-service
- scan
- bar code
- overdue
- fine
- QR code
- lecture
- literature
- available
- make a reservation

In the Canteen

- canteen
- semester
- starve
- nutritious
- on a regular basis
- muscular
- promote
- arouse one's awareness
- pizza
- spaghetti

College Life

- get accustomed to
- schedule
- keyword
- obey
- cultivate
- relatively
- limited
- sign up for
- balance

Part 2 Lead-in

Li Hua and Wang Xia are two freshmen of a vocational college. They are very excited about their college life and they plan to join student societies. They borrow books from the library and talk about their college life.

Part 3 Dialogs

Dialog 1 The Student Society

(On their way to the library, Li Hua and Wang Xia pass a notice board where there are many posters of student societies on it.)

扫码听

Li Hua: Hey, look at this! Student societies are gonna recruit next week!

Wang Xia: Wow, there are so many of them. Let me see.

Li Hua: I'm looking for some sports society... Yeah, this one, the baseball club!

Wang Xia: Baseball? I don't even know you can play baseball!

Li Hua: No, I don't. I've been planning to learn it for so long but haven't started it yet. Are you interested in it? Do you wanna join it with me?

Wang Xia: Well, actually I prefer the yoga club and get some stretches.

Li Hua: That's okay. And I also wanna join the guitar society, but this is an advanced one and they will interview the applicants. I don't know if I can make it because I'm not that good at playing it.

Wang Xia: Just have a try, or else you may regret it. You never know your potential.

Li Hua: You're right. I wanna get one week to practice before the interview.

Wang Xia: The debate society seems interesting as well. You can train your logic in the debate society and they have debate contests every Friday.

Li Hua: Every week? I' m afraid that it takes a lot of time to prepare.

Wang Xia: Don't worry. It is said that you don't need to join in every debate. But they will pick the best debater every month. I guess chances are slim if you don't take an active part in it. And they're gonna hold a debate next weekend to select some debaters from the applicants.

Li Hua: That makes sense.

Wang Xia: You know what, how about we help each other to practice since we both have an interview? I could be your listener and help you play the guitar, and you could help me practice debating.

Li Hua: Wonderful!

Notes

1. I prefer the yoga club and get some stretches.
我想加入瑜伽俱乐部，做一些拉伸运动。
2. I also wanna join the guitar society, but this is an advanced one and they will interview the applicants.
我也想参加吉他社团，但这是一个高级社团，他们要面试申请者。
3. I guess chances are slim if you don't take an active part in it.
如果不积极参与的话，获评最佳辩手的概率估计很小。

Dialog 2 Borrowing and Returning Books

扫码听

(Li Hua and Wang Xia are in the library. Li wants to borrow some books and Wang wants to return the books borrowed before.)

Wang Xia: I have some books to return to the library.

Li Hua: You could use the self-service machine over there.

Wang Xia: Oops. There must be something wrong with the machine. It doesn't work when I scan the bar code.

Li Hua: Don't worry. Let's go to the service desk.

(Li and Wang walk to the service desk.)

Librarian: Good morning. What can I do for you?

Wang Xia: Good morning. I wanna return these books but the self-service machine doesn't work. Here are the books.

Librarian: Okay, let me see... I'm afraid this one is a week overdue. You need to pay a fine of ¥5.

Wang Xia: Sorry, I must have got the time wrong. May I pay by WeChat?

Librarian: Sure, just scan the QR code over there.

Wang Xia: Okay.

(After a while)

Li Hua: I wanna borrow the book mentioned by the professor in yesterday's lecture.

Wang Xia: I remember it's a book about 19th century literature. Maybe we can find it in the literature section on the second floor.

Li Hua: Let me just search for it from the self-service machine. There it is!

It says four of them are not in the library with only one book available on the second floor.

Wang Xia: Perhaps next time you could make a reservation first.

Li Hua: What do you mean by making a reservation?

Wang Xia: Just search for the book you want on the website of our library. If we have it, you can reserve it and choose a date to pick it up. If it has been borrowed by others, you can make a reservation as well, and the website will send you a message if the book is returned.

Li Hua: That saves a lot of time!

(They have got the book on the second floor.)

Li Hua: Can I use the self-service machine to borrow the book?

Wang Xia: Sure. You just need to put your student ID card on this area, scan the bar code on the first page, and the book is under your borrowing list.

Li Hua: That's really convenient!

Notes

1. I'm afraid this one is a week overdue.
   抱歉，这本书超期一周了。
2. It says four of them are not in the library with only one book available on the second floor.
   系统显示有四本不在馆，只有一本在二楼可借。
3. If we have it, you can reserve it and choose a date to pick it up.
   如果我们图书馆有这本书，你可以预约择日来取。

Dialog 3 In the Canteen

(After borrowing and returning books, Li Hua and Wang Xia are on their way to the canteen, talking about where to eat for lunch.)

扫码听

Li Hua: I'm very hungry now.

Wang Xia: Me too. But I can't decide which canteen to go to for lunch.

Li Hua: Well, The food in Canteen 1 is more traditional. Canteen 2 is newly opened this semester, so people are not quite sure about its taste yet. It's relatively modern, serving fast food.

Wang Xia: I remember there's a third one, right?

Li Hua: Yes. The third one is more like a café. It only provides drinks and simple meals. I don't think it's a good choice since we're starving now.

Wang Xia: Well, how about we try the new one? The food in canteen 1 is delicious and nutritious, but we've eaten there for three days.

Li Hua: Great. Let's try something new. Canteen 2 is just down the street. We'll be there in 3 minutes.

(They arrived at the canteen and ordered food. While eating, they are talking about their plans for the weekend.)

Wang Xia: Do you have any plans for the weekend?

Li Hua: Sure. I'm going to the gym and do some workout. I work out on a regular basis to keep fit.

Wang Xia: I guess that's why you're so muscular.

Li Hua: How about you?

Wang Xia: I'm going to the music festival.

Li Hua: Sounds exciting! It is so difficult to get the ticket!

Wang Xia: Absolutely! Besides, I've signed up for the volunteer activity this Sunday.

Li Hua: You mean the activity that promotes bird protection?

Wang Xia: Yeah.

Li Hua: I signed up for it as well. That's meaningful, right? We always suggest protecting the wildlife, but seldom think about how to protect birds, our nearest neighbors in the city.

Wang Xia: That's true. I hope this activity would arouse people's awareness. Oh, by the way, the noodles taste great here! I think we could come here to eat more often.

Li Hua: Sure. My pizza is also wonderful. I wanna try the spaghetti next time.

Notes

1. Canteen 2 is newly opened this semester, so people are not quite sure about its taste yet. It's relatively modern, serving fast food.

   2 号食堂是这学期新开的，大家还不太确定它的口味如何。这是一家相对新式的餐厅，供应快餐。

2. I work out on a regular basis to keep fit.

   我定期健身以保持身体健康。

3. We always suggest protecting the wildlife, but seldom think about how to protect birds, our nearest neighbors in the city.

   我们常说保护野生动物，但很少想到去保护鸟类，它们是我们在城市中的近邻。

Part 4 Passage

College Life

College life is a new chapter for you. You need to get accustomed to living with people from all over the country, deciding on your own, and scheduling your own time. Here are some tips that may be of help to your new journey.

A good relationship with your roommates will give you a wonderful experience of college life. Your roommates may come from all over the country, having different living and eating habits. As you know, respect is a keyword when we get along with people. Besides, it would be better if you set some rules together and obey them.

Unit 1

It might be the first time that you've left home and lived in another city. There are many things you have to decide on your own. It is a great opportunity for you to cultivate independence. However, with relatively limited social experience, you need to ask your parents' suggestions for things you cannot decide or of great importance before determination.

There are various societies and activities that you are interested in, but you may not take part in all of them. It is also important to balance your time spent on hobbies and studies. Going to the library is always a good choice, whether to prepare for your examination or to enlarge your reading.

译文：大学生活

大学是人生的新篇章。你需要适应跟来自全国各地的同学住在一起、自己做决定和规划时间。以下是一些小贴士，或许对你的新“旅程”会有所帮助。

良好的舍友关系会给大学生活带来良好的体验。你的室友也许来自全国各地，有着不同的生活和饮食习惯。要知道，人与人之间相处，重要的是尊重。此外，你跟舍友可以一起制定一些规则并共同遵守。

大学也许是你第一次离家去异乡生活，有很多事情需要自己做决定。这是一个培养独立能力的好机会。然而，由于社会经验不足，对于那些你无法自己决定的抑或非常重要的事情，还是先征询下父母的建议吧。

校园里有诸多你感兴趣的学生社团和活动，但你或许无法一一参与，平衡好用在兴趣爱好和学习上的时间非常重要。去图书馆是一个不错的选择，可以准备考试，也可以扩大阅读面。

Part 5 Exercises

Task 1 Match the words or phrases with the pictures.

1

regret

2

notice board

3

stretch

4

lecture

5

canteen

Task 2 The five students pick different interest groups. Please choose their possible reasons.

Possible reasons:

enhance hands-on ability

cultivate innovative thinking

promote reading and writing skills

get some stretches and build up body

train logic and improve communication skills

Name	Interest Group	Reason
Wang Xia	yoga club	
Zhang Ming	speech group	
Zhou Yingying	literature group	
Ethan	science club	
Zoe	paper-cut group	

Task 3 List five books you want to read and search them on your college's library website to see if they are available.

Book Title	Available or Not

Task 4 Role Play

Talk about your plans with your partner. It could be your weekend plan, semester plan, holiday plan, or year plan... Please make your description as detailed as possible.

Unit 1

Part 6 Self-evaluation

评价项目	评价内容	自我诊断	改进措施
语言知识	I learn many useful words and expressions about campus life.	☐ Identifying ☐ Understanding ☐ Mastering	
认知能力	I know the steps of borrowing and returning books from the library.	☐ Distinction ☐ Merit ☐ Pass ☐ Fail	
沟通能力	I can talk about my campus life, such as weekend plans, student societies, etc.	☐ Distinction ☐ Merit ☐ Pass ☐ Fail	
文化意识	I get to learn about the spirit of China's youth in the new era.	☐ Increasing ☐ Developing ☐ Weakening	

Part 7 Culture

Youth of China in the New Era (Excerpt)

The State Council Information Office of the People's Republic of China

April 2022

(from *http://www.scio.gov.cn/zfbps/ndhf/2022n/202304/t20230407_710480.html*)

A country will be full of hope and can look forward to a bright prospect when its young generation has ideals, abilities, and a strong sense of responsibility. The future of China and the future of the wider world both belong to the young.

In the future, the young Chinese generation will "with their youthfulness, create a vibrant family, country, nation, human community, Earth and the universe". They will make their youthful dreams come true.

In the future, with successive efforts from one generation of young people to the next, China will scale new heights in every dimension, achieving economic, political, cultural, ethical, social, and eco-environmental progress. The Chinese people will enjoy a happier and healthier life and the Chinese nation will become a proud and active member of the community of nations. The great Chinese Dream will eventually become a reality.

The future of the world is related to the destiny of every young person, and it also depends on the efforts that every young person makes. If young people from all countries unite for the common goal, uphold justice, work in harmony, help each other, conduct consultation as equals, and commit to openness and innovation, we will be able to steer clear of strife and war, build a "global village" that pursues peaceful development and harmony, jointly create a future of prosperity, health, safety, mutual respect, mutual learning, and shared benefits, and ultimately realize the common dream of all of humanity.

China's youth stand ready to work with their counterparts from all over the world and contribute their wisdom and strength to building a global community of shared future and a better world.

Unit 2

Learning in College

扫码看

Learning Objectives

After learning this unit, you should be able to:

1. get familiar with the words and expressions concerning majors and courses in college;
2. give a brief introduction to majors and studies in English;
3. know that China's higher education has made great progress, especially vocational education.

Unit 2

Part 1 Topic Words and Expressions

扫码听

Talking about Courses

- major
- course
- adjust
- compulsory course
- specialized basic course
- professional skill course
- public basic course
- freshman
- semester
- fascinated

Choosing Elective Courses

- elective
- cut-off date
- select
- in that case
- online course
- flexible
- enroll
- appreciation
- improve
- offline

Training Courses

- practical training course
- arrange
- theoretical course
- sophomore
- accounting
- set up accounts
- accounting voucher
- instruct
- register
- otherwise

How to Study Effectively

- effectively
- initiative
- academic demands
- motivate
- course load
- crucial
- diagram
- table
- mind map
- visual timeline
- quiz

Part 2 Lead-in

Some students of different majors and grades are members of the college basketball club. Before the club activities, they discuss their respective majors and courses.

Part 3 Dialogs

Dialog 1 Talking about Courses

扫码听

(Tan Fei and Xiao Qi are talking about the courses they are taking.)

Tan Fei: Long time no see. How have you been these days?

Xiao Qi: Fine. I've just been very busy lately.

Tan Fei: It's just the beginning of the term. What are you doing?

Xiao Qi: As a computer major student, I have ten courses so I'm trying to adjust to the new learning life.

Tan Fei: Ten courses? Why did you take so many courses?

Xiao Qi: There are five compulsory courses this term for my major, that is, three specialized basic courses and two professional skill courses. Besides,

I have to take three public basic courses, such as College English course.

Tan Fei: What're another two courses?

Xiao Qi: Do you forget it? All the freshmen have to choose at least two elective courses next week.

Tan Fei: Really? I completely forgot about it.

Xiao Qi: How many courses are you taking this semester?

Tan Fei: I'm taking six courses now, three art major courses and three other courses. One of them is Basic Computer Science. I think it will be useful for my major. In addition, two more elective courses will be chosen next week.

Xiao Qi: The college offers a total of 60 electives. Which ones are you going to take?

Tan Fei: Well, to be honest, I haven't thought about it, but I'm interested in English-related courses. What about you?

Xiao Qi: I've always been fascinated with the new development of artificial intelligence, so I may choose electives related to science and technology.

Tan Fei: It must be meaningful and fulfilling this term.

Notes

1. As a computer major student, I have ten courses so I'm trying to adjust to the new learning life.
作为一名计算机专业的学生，我有十门课程，所以我正在努力适应新的学习生活。

2. There are five compulsory courses this term for my major, that is, three specialized basic courses and two professional skill courses.

这学期我有五门专业必修课——三门专业基础课和两门专业技能课。

3. I've always been fascinated with the new development of artificial intelligence, so I may choose electives related to science and technology.

一直以来我对人工智能的新发展很感兴趣，所以我可能会选择与科技相关的选修课。

Dialog 2 Choosing Elective Courses

扫码听

(Li Hua and Wang Xia are talking about how to choose an elective course.)

Li Hua: Do you know that we can choose the elective courses?

Wang Xia: Oh, I don't know. When is the cut-off date?

Li Hua: Next Friday. You should first think about which course you love to select.

Wang Xia: I've no idea. Do you know what elective courses the college is offering this term?

Li Hua: I've got the list. Here you are.

Wang Xia: Thank you. You know, I already have eight compulsory courses this term, so the elective course will make me busier.

Li Hua: Well, in that case, why not try an online elective course?

Wang Xia: That's great! It is flexible enough for me to take an online course.

Li Hua: It's true. Taking online courses, we can decide when it is the suitable time to have them.

Wang Xia: Oh, I want to enroll in this course.

Li Hua: Which one? The English Films Appreciation?

Wang Xia: Yes. I guess I can watch many English films in the class.

Li Hua: It sounds like an interesting course.

Wang Xia: It must be very difficult but it's an online course, so I could watch the video more than once.

Li Hua: I also like watching English movies, but only for entertainment.

Wang Xia: It will be a challenge for me but I hope to improve my English by taking the course.

Li Hua: I'm sure you will.

Wang Xia: Thank you. Which course are you going to take, the offline elective or online elective?

Li Hua: Oh, look at the list of electives. I'm going to choose this one.

Notes

1. You know, I already have eight compulsory courses this term, so the elective course will make me busier.

   要知道，这学期我已经有八门必修课了，所以选修课会让我变得更忙。

2. Which course are you going to take, the offline elective or online elective?

   你打算选哪门课，线下选修课还是线上选修课？

Dialog 3 Training Courses

扫码听

(Lin Wei didn't attend the club activity this week. Hu Jun calls him.)

Hu Jun: Hello, this is Hu Jun. Is that Lin Wei speaking?

Lin Wei: Yeah, this is Lin Wei speaking.

Hu Jun: You didn't attend the club activity this week. What's the matter? Are you OK?

Lin Wei: I'm fine. I took part in the practical training course of my major this week, so I couldn't attend our club activities.

Hu Jun: Wow, that sounds interesting! I heard that practical training courses are arranged for each major from the second year of college. I'm looking forward to it next year!

Lin Wei: Instead of taking more theoretical courses, students have to take a series of practical training courses in order to improve their practical abilities.

Hu Jun: So you sophomores begin the practical learning from this term.

Lin Wei: Yes. As a student of accounting major, the main task in this week is to learn how to set up accounts.

Hu Jun: Specifically, how did you practice?

Lin Wei: First, the teacher explained how to fill in the accounting voucher and asked us to do it in practice. Next, the teacher instructed us to register various detailed accounts. Finally, team members should check accounts with each other and make corrections.

Hu Jun: The training course is closely related to your major.

Lin Wei: Exactly. You'd better learn the theoretical courses well in the first year, otherwise you will find it hard to cope with the practical training the next year.

Hu Jun: Thank you for your advice. I'll try to do well in my theoretical courses.

Notes

1. I took part in the practical training course of my major this week, so I couldn't go to attend our club activities.
   这周我参加了专业实训课程，所以无法去参加社团活动。
2. Instead of taking more theoretical courses, students have to take a series of practical training courses in order to improve their practical abilities.
   我们学校的学生必须上一系列的实训课程，而非更多的理论课程，以此提高他们的实践能力。

3. First, the teacher explained how to fill in the accounting voucher and asked us to do it in practice.
   首先，老师讲解如何填写会计凭证，并让我们进行实践。
4. Next, the teacher instructed us to register various detailed accounts.
   接下来，老师指导我们登记各种明细账户。

Part 4 Passage

How to Study Effectively

Most college students are confused about how to study effectively. So, taking the initiative to discover effective study techniques on your own is a wise move. By taking control of your learning process, you can better prepare yourself for the academic demands of college life.

First, know your goals and values. Acknowledging your goals is the first step to achieve success. Recognizing what you are trying to achieve by pursuing an education can help illuminate your values, and you can use those values to motivate yourself as you work toward your goals.

Second, make a study schedule. How much time you need to study in college will depend on your course load, your learning style, and your personal interests. Effective time management is essential. Once you have a schedule, stick to it.

Third, go to class and listen in class. Class is often the primary place of learning. If a professor is going to introduce a new topic, he or she will often detail that topic in class and may provide information unavailable in the textbook. Pay attention, take notes, and don't be afraid to ask questions if there's something you don't understand.

Fourth, try different study techniques. As many successful college students have mentioned, you could study for exams by exploring different study methods and discovering what works best for you. For example, try drawing diagrams or tables to help you understand some information. Creating a mind map or a visual timeline could also be helpful.

Fifth, quiz yourself. Reading a page of your textbook over and over again is helpful, but repeated re-reading is not the best way to keep the information in your mind. If you want to make sure you really understand the material, you should test yourself on it. Try testing yourself by looking at past exams, making flash cards, or having a study buddy ask you questions. It will help you in the long run.

Last, take care of your health. Maintaining your mental and physical health is crucial to reaching your goals. For example, a lack of sleep can disrupt your body's ability to function.

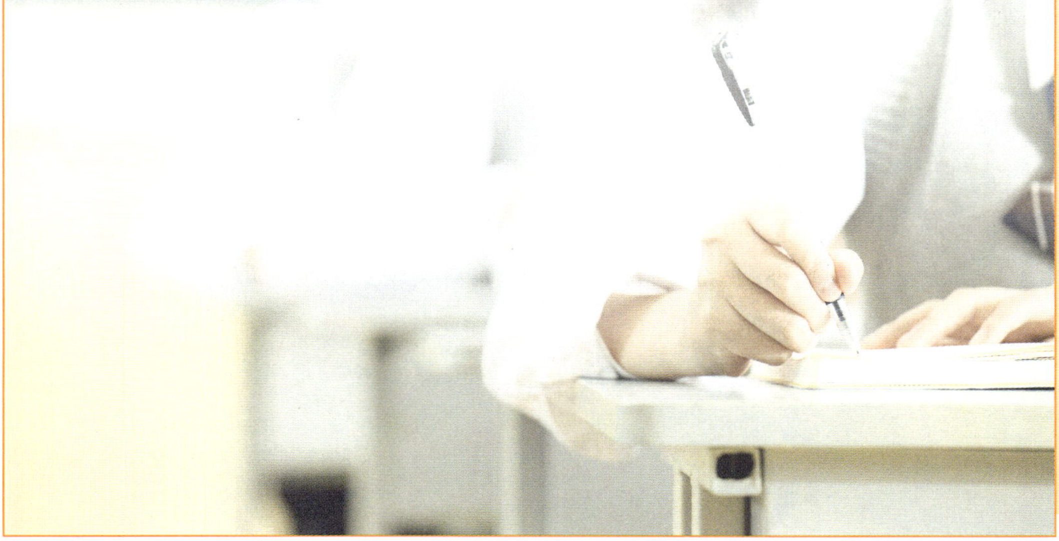

Unit 2

译文：如何有效学习

大多数大学生对如何有效地学习感到困惑。所以主动去发现有效的学习技巧是一个明智之举。通过控制学习过程，你可以更好地为大学的学业要求做好准备。

首先，了解你的目标和价值观。确认目标是取得成功的第一步。认识到你想通过接受教育来实现什么，有助于阐明你的价值观；你可以用这样的价值观来激励自己朝着目标努力。

第二，制订学习计划。在大学需要多少时间来学习取决于你的课程量、学习方式和个人兴趣。有效的时间管理必不可少。一旦你有了学习计划，就要坚持下去。

第三，上课和听讲。课堂通常是学习的主要场所。如果教授要介绍一个新主题，他们通常会在课堂上进行详细介绍，可能会包括课本上没有涵盖的信息。认真听讲，做笔记，如果有不懂的地方，不要害怕问问题。

第四，尝试不同的学习技巧。正如许多成功的大学生所提到的，你可以探索不同的学习方法并发现最适合你的方法。例如，试着画图表或表格来帮助你理解一些信息。创建思维导图或视觉时间轴也会有所帮助。

第五，自我测试。一遍又一遍地阅读一页书对学习有所帮助，但是反复重读并不是把信息牢牢记在脑子里的最好方法。如果想确保你真的理解了材料，你应该测试一下自己。可以通过试着回顾过去的考试，制作卡片，或者让学习伙伴向你提问题的方式来测试自己。从长远看，这对你是有帮助的。

最后，照顾好你的身体。保持身心健康对实现目标至关重要。例如，睡眠不足会破坏身体机能。

Part 5 Exercises

Task 1 Match the course categories with the specific courses.

Course Categories	Courses
1. major	A. P. E. , College English (for all majors)
2. elective course	B. Accounting Practical Skill Course (for Accounting majors)
3. compulsory course	C. Computer Application Technology, Mechanical Manufacture, etc.
4. public basic course	D. International Economics (for International Trade majors)
5. professional skill course	E. Chinese Martial Arts Course, Film Art Appreciation Course, etc.

1. ____________ 2. ____________ 3. ____________

4. ____________ 5. ____________

Task 2 The following is a list of elective courses offered by a college this term. Please help the students choose their preferred elective courses.

The List of Elective Courses	
1	Chinese Calligraphy
2	Mathematical Modeling Method
3	Nutrition and Health
4	Basketball Tactics
5	Appreciation of Dramas
6	Introduction to Psychology

Application Form		
Name	Hobbies	Elective Course
Xiao Qi	Movies	
Jay Wang	Mental health	
Tan Fei	Sports	
Teresa Liu	Chinese traditional culture	
Li Qing	Mathematics	

Task 3 Teresa and Jay are two students majoring in Accounting. They are having the training course these days. Please fill in the blanks to show the training steps according to Dialogue 3.

Step 1 The teacher explains ________ and asks students to do it in practice.

Step 2 The teacher instructs students ________.

Step 3 Students in the same team should ________ and make corrections.

Task 4 Role Play

Student A: Imagine you are a freshman in a college.

Ask questions about the categories of courses.

Student B: Imagine you are a sophomore having the same major as Student A.

Answer Student A's question and introduce how to learn the major efficiently.

Change roles and try the role play again.

Part 6 Self-evaluation

评价项目	评价内容	自我诊断	改进措施
语言知识	I learn many common words and expressions about majors and courses.	□ Identifying □ Understanding □ Mastering	
认知能力	I know the categories and features of different courses.	□ Distinction □ Merit □ Pass □ Fail	
沟通能力	I can briefly introduce majors, courses and learning technigues in English.	□ Distinction □ Merit □ Pass □ Fail	
文化意识	I get to learn about China's great achievements in higher education, especially vocational education.	□ Increasing □ Developing □ Weakening	

Unit 2

Part 7 Culture

Across China:Vocational Education Turns Youngsters into World Champions (Excerpt)

Xinhua | Updated: 2023-06-26

(from *https://www.chinadaily.com.cn*)

GUANGZHOU, June 25(Xinhua)—Guangdong Machinery Technician College may not sound like an elite educational institute, but the vocational college in South China's economic powerhouse Guangdong province has produced 10 gold medalists in the World Skills Competition over the last 10 years.

Hailed as the "Skills Olympics", the World Skills Competition is a global event that celebrates vocational skill excellence.

Among these champions is Zhou Chujie, who won the gold medal in the CNC milling competition at the World Skills Competition 2022 Special Edition. Now as a teacher at the college, the 24-year-old Zhou said he discovered his passion for technical work during a visit to a numerically-controlled workshop in junior high school.

...

With that goal in mind, Zhou enrolled in the machinery technician college, specializing in CNC milling as his major. After tenaciously honing his skills, he stood out among his peers, earning the opportunity to represent China and eventually winning the crown in the World Skills Competition 2022 Special Edition.

Dubbed the "world's factory", China has long put vocational education high on its policy agenda, establishing the largest vocational education system in the world.

Unit 3

Shopping

扫码看

Learning Objectives

After learning this unit, you should be able to:

1. get familiar with the words and expressions concerning shopping online and at brick-and-mortar stores;
2. select goods according to your own wishes, ask price, bargain, and return or exchange stuff;
3. know that China has made a huge contribution in promoting globalization.

Unit 3

Part 1 Topic Words and Expressions

扫码听

Shopping Online

- attend
- wedding
- review
- fashion icon
- compliment
- negative
- comment
- delivery
- sparkling
- positive
- afford

Returning and Exchanging

- counter
- vamp
- misplace
- refund
- original
- purchasing date
- regular
- exception
- exchange

Shopping at a Brick-and-mortar Store

- accompany
- high heel
- fashionable
- storeroom
- fit
- suitable
- discount
- tag price
- receipt

Community Group Purchasing

- purchase
- witness
- indicate
- resident
- compound
- bulk
- convenient
- coupon
- pattern
- deceptive
- after-sale service

Part 2 Lead-in

Li Na and Wang Xia are two freshmen of a college. They are close friends. Li Na is going home to attend a wedding on the coming May Day. She wants to buy a dress and a pair of shoes and is eager to get some suggestions from Wang Xia.

Part 3 Dialogs

Dialog 1 Shopping Online

扫码听

(Li Na is thinking of buying a dress and a pair of shoes for attending a wedding and Wang Xia gives her some advice.)

Li Na: Hello, Wang Xia.

Wang Xia: Hi, Li Na.

Li Na: What are you doing?

Wang Xia: Nothing. Just reviewing the lessons we have learned.

Li Na: Great! Well, can you do me a favor?

Wang Xia: What is it?

Li Na: I'm going to attend a wedding on the coming May Day and I'm thinking of buying a dress and a pair of shoes.

Wang Xia: Really?

Li Na: Yes, so I want to know your suggestions. In my mind, you are a fashion icon.

Wang Xia: Thank you for your compliment. I think you can buy the dress online and the shoes offline.

Li Na: Good idea. Which website do you usually shop on?

Wang Xia: I usually shop on Taobao. Of course, you can also shop on JD and Vipshop. They are also popular shopping sites among people.

Li Na: Let's try Taobao first.

(Li Na clicks on Taobao App and begins searching for dresses.)

Li Na: How about this dress?

Wang Xia: It's quite cheap.

Li Na: That's why I choose it. You can never get a dress like this in a store with such a price.

Wang Xia: But I think it doesn't fit your body type. Besides, there are so many negative comments about the slow delivery, and poor quality.

Li Na: OK. Let's give it up. How about this red one?

Wang Xia: No, it's too sparkling. It doesn't fit you, either.

Li Na: Well, what about the pink one?

Wang Xia: Seems good. It's a little bit simple but formal enough for a wedding.

Li Na: The most comments are positive, although it's a bit expensive.

Wang Xia: The stuff with good quality is usually expensive.

Li Na: But it's okay. I can afford it. Thanks for your help, Wang Xia.

Wang Xia: Don't mention it.

Notes

1. Thank you for your compliment.
   谢谢你的夸奖。
2. Which website do you usually shop on?
   你通常在哪个网站购物?
3. But I think it doesn't fit your body type.
   但我认为它不适合你的体型。

Dialog 2 Shopping at a Brick-and-mortar Store (Physical Store)

扫码听

(Wang Xia and Li Na go to a shopping mall to buy shoes on Saturday.)

Li Na: Hi, Wang Xia. I have received the dress I bought on Taobao with your help. It fits me well. I like it very much.

Wang Xia: I'm glad to hear that.

Li Na: Could you do me a favor again? That is to buy a pair of shoes with me this Saturday.

Wang Xia: With pleasure.

Li Na: Great!

(Li Na and Wang Xia are in a shopping centre on Saturday.)

Saleswoman: Good morning, ladies. Welcome to CELLE. How can I help you?

Li Na: Yes, I'm looking for some shoes for my cousin's wedding party. Something with high heels.

Saleswoman: Have you ever tried this brand? The shoes of this brand are really fashionable. What do you think of this pair? They look very nice.

Li Na: Yes, the pair you mentioned are very attractive, but I prefer the red pair over there.

Saleswoman: Yes, what size do you take?

Li Na: I often take Size 37. Please give me a pair with 7 cm high heels.

Saleswoman: Yes, Miss. Please give me a few minutes, I'll check in the storeroom.

(A few minutes later, the saleswoman comes back with a pair of red high-heel shoes in Size 37. Li Na tries it on.)

Saleswoman: Do they fit you all right?

Li Na: Yes, they fit me perfectly. How about this pair of shoes, Wang Xia?

Wang Xia: They look very nice! But what dress will you come with these shoes?

Li Na: The pink dress I bought online.

Wang Xia: I think the white pair is more suitable. Do you like this color? You would be more attractive at the wedding party with the white pair.

Li Na: OK. Let me have a try. Could you please bring me the white pair?

Saleswoman: All right, just a moment please, I'll check in the storeroom.

(Several minutes later, the saleswoman comes back with the right shoes.)

Saleswoman: Here you are. Have a seat and try this pair.

Li Na: Thank you.

Saleswoman: Go ahead and walk around.

Wang Xia: Wow, they look great. Let's take this pair of shoes.

Li Na: Yes, I think so. This pair of shoes will match perfectly with my dress. How much are they?

Saleswoman: They cost ¥298. That is a reasonable price for such good shoes.

Li Na: Do you give any discount?

Saleswoman: Are you a member of our store? We offer a 5% discount to members.

Li Na: Yes, I'm a member of your store.

Saleswoman: Then, the tag price is ¥ 298, so 5% off is ¥ 283.

Li Na: Great. I'll take them.

Saleswoman: They look great on you. Nice choice. How would you like to pay? Card, WeChat or Alipay?

Li Na: I'll pay by Alipay.

Saleswoman: Here is your receipt. I hope you will like your new shoes.

Li Na: Thank you. Goodbye.

Notes

1. Could you do me a favor again?

   你能再帮我一个忙吗?

2. I think the white pair is more suitable.

   我觉得这双白色的更适合。

3. Do you give any discount?

   你们打折吗?

Dialog 3 Returning and Exchanging

扫码听

(Li Na comes into CELLE counter. She wants to return the shoes she bought about two months ago.)

Saleswoman: Hi, can I help you?

Li Na: Yes, I would like to return this pair of shoes.

Saleswoman: May I ask what's wrong with them.

Li Na: The Vamp.

Saleswoman: I'm sorry to hear that. May I have your receipt?

Unit 3

Li Na: I must have misplaced my receipt. Is it possible to get a refund without the original receipt?

Saleswoman: Don't worry. Tell me your purchasing date. I'll check the sales records.

Li Na: Thank you. I bought it on a Saturday before May Day.

Saleswoman: I found it. You bought it on April 29th.

Li Na: So, can I get a refund?

Saleswoman: There's a little trouble, Miss.

Li Na: What's the problem?

Saleswoman: It will be a bit more difficult to return the shoes and get a refund without the original receipt.

Li Na: I'm a regular customer here. Can you make an exception for me?

Saleswoman: Well, let me talk to the manager for a moment.

(Several minutes later)

Saleswoman: Miss, our manager said you can exchange this pair of shoes for another pair with the same or lower price.

Li Na: OK. I choose to exchange. Thank you very much.

Saleswoman: You are welcome. Now, you can choose a pair of new shoes...

Notes

1. I would like to return this pair of shoes.

   我想退掉这双鞋子。

2. May I have your receipt?

   我可以看一下您的收据吗？

3. I'm a regular customer here. Can you make an exception for me?

   我是这里的常客，你能给我破例一次吗？

Part 4 Passage

Community Group Purchasing

In recent years, China is witnessing a new type of online shopping fever—community group purchasing, which was originally introduced from foreign countries but is now widely popular all over China. As the name indicates, community group purchasing allows a group of residents within the same apartment compound to get discounts by buying together in bulk.

Community group purchasing is very convenient and it can save people a lot of money. Customers can not only buy various kinds of goods in the way, but also purchase tickets, coupons and services at lower cost.

Popular as it is, it also has some problems. Since community group purchasing is nothing more than another form of online shopping, the nature of it is no different from other online shopping patterns. Problems that exist in online shopping also can be found in group purchasing, like deceptive advertisement, poor quality goods, and the incomplete after-sale service.

We should treat community group purchasing as a way of shopping and nothing more. We must be careful not to buy something we don't need only to follow the fashion.

译文：社区团购

近年来，中国正在经历一种新型的网上购物热——社区团购，这种模式最初是从国外引入的，但现在在中国非常流行。顾名思义，社区团购允许同一小区的一群居民一起批量购买，从而获得折扣。

社区团购非常方便，它可以为人们节省很多钱。顾客不仅可以通过这种方式购买到各种商品，还可以以更低的价格购买门票、优惠券和服务。

虽然它很受欢迎，但也有一些问题。由于社区团购只不过是另一种形式的网上购物，本质上与其他网上购物模式没有什么不同。网上购物中存在的问题也存在于社区团购中，比如虚假广告、劣质商品、售后服务不完善。

我们应该将社区团购视为一种购物方式，仅此而已。我们必须小心，不要为了赶时髦而买我们不需要的东西。

Part 5 Exercises

Task 1 Match the shopping websites on the left with their Chinese names on the right. Then discuss with your partner which site(s) do you shop on most.

1. tmall.com	A. 淘宝
2. JD.com	B. 唯品会
3. pinduoduo.com	C. 快手电商
4. taobao.com	D. 当当
5. douyinec.com	E. 京东
6. suning.com	F. 抖音电商
7. kwaixiaodian.com	G. 苏宁易购
8. dangdang.com	H. 天猫
9. vip.com	I. 聚美优品
10. jumei.com	J. 拼多多

Task 2 Read the following situational dialogue. Fill in the blanks with suitable words according dialogue 2.

A: Good morning! How can I 1. __________ you?

B: Good morning! I want to buy a pair of shoes. I like that pair over there.

A: What size do you 2. __________?

B: I often take Size 38.

A: All right. Just a moment please. I'll check in the 3. __________.

(Several minutes later. A comes back with the right shoes.)

A: Here you are. Have a seat and 4. __________ this pair.

B: They look great on me. Any chance of a lower 5. __________ from you?

A: ¥198 is the lowest price.

B: OK. I'll take this pair.

Task 3 Translate the following expressions about returning and exchanging.

1. I'd like to return this pair of shoes.
2. Can I get a refund?
3. I want to exchange this skirt for a different color.
4. May I see your receipt?
5. You arrived just in time. The return period of 7 days ends today.

Task 4 Role Play

Student A: Imagine you are a customer in a physical store.
Ask questions about the return and exchange policies of the store.

Student B: Imagine you are a saleswoman in a physical store.
Answer the customer's questions and try to solve the customer's problem.

Change roles and try the role play again.

Part 6 Self-evaluation

评价项目	评价内容	自我诊断	改进措施
语言知识	I learn many common words and expressions about shopping.	□ Identifying □ Understanding □ Mastering	
认知能力	I know how to shop online and at a brick-and-mortar store.	□ Distinction □ Merit □ Pass □ Fail	
沟通能力	I can use English to bargain for a lower price and communicate with salesperson to return and exchange stuff.	□ Distinction □ Merit □ Pass □ Fail	
文化意识	I get to learn about China's great achievements in promoting globalization.	□ Increasing □ Developing □ Weakening	

Unit 3

Part 7 Culture

China International Import Expo: A "win-win" Approach (Excerpt)

(from *https://www.chinadaily.com.cn*, Updated: 2018–11–13)

Chinese civilization has a history of several thousand years, and has seen many ups and downs throughout history. Chinese people have learned many things through hard lessons. Chinese wisdom is a "win-win" approach and they practice this approach a lot. One of the latest examples is China International Import Expo, a unique and innovative concept. Many countries hold export expos frequently. Every country wants to boost its exports and earn more foreign exchange. But China does things differently.

China International Import Expo has two roles. On the one hand, China wants to help rest of the world enter Chinese market. The visionary leadership has provided enabling environment and conducive policies. As a result, China manufactures quality products at a reasonable price. Therefore, Chinese products are in demand globally. Today, China enjoys

trade surplus with the whole world.

China believes in "win-win" philosophy and wants to provide a fair opportunity to rest of the world to access Chinese market. It may help some of the countries to narrow down the trade gap.

On the other hand, China is one of the biggest importers of some of the goods. The import expo will benefit China in much more competitive imports. Definitely, many countries will try to capture Chinese market by providing better quality and yet competitive in price. It will benefit China import best quality yet at an affordable price. Sure, it will be a "win-win" situation for China as well as for the rest of world.

China International Import Expo will open a new chapter of further development in China. It will become hub of international trade and world will be attracted to Shanghai.

China International Import Expo is a positive step and a clear message that China promotes globalization. It is expected that the rest of world will also appreciate it and be beneficiary of Chinese free and fair trade practices.

Unit 4

Food

扫码看

Learning Objectives

After learning this unit, you should be able to:

1. get familiar with the words and expressions concerning reserving and ordering Chinese and Western food;
2. know how to order in a Chinese restaurant or a Western restaurant;
3. know that China's traditional food is popular with more and more people.

Unit 4

Part 1 Topic Words and Expressions

扫码听

At a Chinese Restaurant

- specific
- cuisine
- mention
- salty
- slightly
- authentic
- reservation
- lounge
- immediately
- as soon as
- take your seat
- menu

Having Western Food

- in advance
- confirm
- arrange
- lemonade
- steak
- Caesar salad
- medium-well
- grilled
- sauce
- dessert

Ordering Sichuan Food

- recommend
- classic
- peanut
- chili pepper
- typical
- sliced beef
- beef offal
- mouth-numbing
- staple food
- steamed bread

Takeout Food

- takeout
- indispensable
- in terms of
- delivery
- precious
- reduce
- ingredient
- abundant
- incomparable
- extra
- imperfect
- verify

Part 2 Lead-in

Li Hua invites his American friend, Jack, to have Chinese food. The next day, Jack treats Li Hua a Western meal.

Part 3 Dialogs

Dialog 1 At a Chinese Restaurant

(Jack came to China the first time, and Li Hua invites him to have Chinese food.)

扫码听

Li Hua: It's time for dinner. Would you like to try Chinese food? I will treat you.

Jack: Thank you. I know Chinese food is very famous, so I want to have a try. But I have no idea about it. Could you tell me what different kinds of Chinese food do you have?

Li Hua: To be specific, Chinese food can be divided into eight big cuisines, or eight styles, such as Shandong cuisine, Guangdong cuisine, Sichuan cuisine and Jiangsu cuisine, etc.

Jack: Could you tell me the differences between the four cuisines you have mentioned?

Unit 4

Li Hua: With pleasure. Generally Shandong cuisine is heavy and a little salty, Guangdong cuisine is a bit light, Sichuan cuisine has a strong and hot taste and Jiangsu cuisine is slightly sweet.

Jack: Great! I like hot food, so I want to try Sichuan food first.

Li Hua: I happen to know a very authentic Sichuan restaurant. Let's go.

(Li Hua and Jack come to the Sichuan restaurant.)

Waiter: Good evening. Welcome to our restaurant. Do you have a reservation?

Li Hua: I'm afraid we haven't. Could you find a table for us?

Waiter: I'm sorry. All the tables have been taken. Would you mind waiting for a while?

Li Hua: How long do you think we'll have to wait?

Waiter: At least 15 minutes I guess. You can have a drink in the lounge while waiting. I'll have you seated immediately as soon as we have a free table.

Li Hua: All right.

Waiter: Come this way, please.

(15 minutes later)

Waiter: I'm sorry to have kept you waiting for so long, gentlemen. Here is a table for two. Would you please take your seats here?

Li Hua: Oh, great. I like to sit here.

Waiter: Here are the menu and drink list. Take your time.

Notes

1. I happen to know a very authentic Sichuan restaurant.
   我碰巧知道一家非常地道的川菜馆。
2. Do you have a reservation?
   您有预定吗？

3. I'll have you seated immediately as soon as we have a free table.

一有空桌，我马上给你们安排座位。

Dialog 2 Ordering Sichuan Food

(Li Hua and Jack are reading the menu. A few minutes later the waiter comes over to them.)

扫码听

Waiter: Excuse me, sir. Are you ready to order?

Jack: I know little about Sichuan food, Li Hua. You order, please.

Li Hua: No problem. (Facing to the waiter) But there are so many dishes on the menu that look fine. Could you recommend me something special?

Waiter: Yes, sir. We have Kung Pao Chicken today. It's our chef's recommendation. It's a classic Sichuan dish made with chicken, peanuts, vegetables and chili peppers.

Li Hua: OK. I'll take it. What about Sliced Beef and Ox Tongue in Chilli Sauce?

Waiter: It's also a typical Sichuan dish. Sliced Beef and Ox Tongue in Chilli Sauce served cold or at room temperature, is made of thinly sliced beef and beef offal. It's spicy and mouth-numbing.

Li Hua: I'll have it.

Waiter: What about Mapo Tofu and Twice Cooked Pork?

Li Hua: That's a good idea. Any staple food?

Waiter: We have rice and steamed bread.

Li Hua: Just two bowls of rice.

Waiter: Sir, you'd like Kung Pao Chicken, Sliced Beef and Ox Tongue in Chilli Sauce, Mapo Tofu, Twice Cooked Pork, and two bowls of rice.

Li Hua: Yes, exactly.

Unit 4

Waiter: Sir, your dishes will take about 20 minutes to prepare. While waiting, would you have something to drink?

Li Hua: Jasmine tea, please. What would you like to drink, Jack?

Jack: A can of coke, thanks.

(About two hours later, the waiter comes to Li Hua and Jack.)

Waiter: Is everything okay here?

Li Hua: We're good.

Waiter: Anything else I can bring you?

Li Hua: No, that's fine. We're about done here. May we have the bill?

Waiter: Sure.

(Several minutes later, the waiter comes back with the bill.)

Waiter: This is your bill. That comes to ¥226.

Li Hua: I'll get this.

Jack: Thanks for your treat, Li Hua.

Notes

1. Are you ready to order?
   您准备好点菜了吗？
2. What would you like to drink?
   您想喝点什么？
3. We're about done here. May we have the bill?
   我们差不多吃完了，请给我们账单好吗？

Dialog 3 Having Western Food

扫码听

Jack: Let's go for Western food tonight. I'll treat.

Li Hua: That's great. Thank you.

Jack: I'll make a reservation in advance this time.

Li Hua: Good idea.

(Jack searches the phone number of the Western restaurant online and makes a phone call.)

Hostess: This is PULANER. May I help you?

Jack: Yes. I'd like to reserve a table for two this evening.

Hostess: All right. And what time do you want?

Jack: 6:30 p.m.

Hostess: Let's confirm. We've got a table for two at 6:30 this evening. May I have your name, please?

Jack: Jack Green.

Hostess: OK. Mr. Green. We'll see you this evening.

Jack: By the way, can you arrange a table by the window?

Hostess: No problem. I'll arrange one for you.

Jack: That's great. Thank you. Bye.

Hostess: It's my pleasure. Bye.

(Jack and Li Hua come to the restaurant at 6:30 p.m.)

Waiter: Welcome to PULANER. May I help you?

Jack: Yes, I have a reservation for tonight, under the name of Jack Green.

Waiter: Hello, Mr. Green. Your table is ready. This way, please.

(After Jack and Li Hua sit down)

Waiter: Sir, would you like a drink before the main course?

Jack: Yes.

Unit 4

Waiter: So, what do you want for drink?

Li Hua: I'd like to have a glass of orange juice.

Jack: I'd like a lemonade, please.

Waiter: Sir, this is your drinks.

Jack: Please show me your menu.

Waiter: This is our menu. May I take your order now?

Li Hua: I'd like to order Italian steaks and a Caesar salad.

Waiter: How would you like your steak, sir?

Li Hua: Medium-well, please.

Waiter: OK, noted. How about you, sir?

Jack: I want grilled mushroom sauce and a bowl of pumpkin soup.

Waiter: Please wait. We will prepare it for you right now.

(About an hour later, Jack and Li Hua finish their meal.)

Jack: Waiter, we want to order some dessert.

Waiter: OK, sir, for dessert, we have lemon tart, apple pie, cream pie and ice cream. What do you want to order?

Li Hua: I'll go for lemon tart.

Jack: I'd like an apple pie.

Waiter: Please wait a minute.

(Several minutes later, the waiter comes back with the ordered dessert.)

Waiter: Here you are.

Jack: Thank you.

Waiter: Is there anything I can help you?

Li Hua: Not yet. Thanks.

Notes

1. I'd like to reserve a table for two this evening.
   我想预订一张今晚两个人的桌位。
2. Can you arrange a table by the window?
   你能安排一张靠窗的桌子吗?
3. How would you like your steak, sir?
   先生，您的牛排要几分熟?
4. We want to order some dessert.
   我们想点甜点。

Part 4 Passage

Takeout Food

Nowadays, ordering takeout has become an indispensable part of people's life. It can not only save us a lot of cooking time, but also give us more freedom and choice in terms of diet structure. With the increase of takeout orders, many takeout delivery platforms have appeared one after another. Ordering takeout is far more convenient than cooking at home.

Speaking of the advantages of takeout, the first is to save time. Nowadays, people have become busier and the time for family dinner has become very precious. Moreover, some people work overtime at night and have no time to cook. Therefore, takeout not only solves the problem of dinner that needs to be solved, but also reduces the time of cooking. Besides, ordering takeout is also very convenient. You can avoid the trouble of going out to buy ingredients and cooking them. You can order takeaway through the Internet and you can also have delicious food at home.

In addition, ordering takeout can also provide more choices according to different diet structures. Everyone has different tastes when it comes to food. Some people like hotpot and some people like Sushi. With ordering takeout, everyone can satisfy their own taste. As long as you want to eat something, you can order it directly from the takeaway delivery platforms. Also, when it comes to the variety of food, the type of ordering takeout is also more abundant than cooking.

Of course, there are also some disadvantages of takeout. Generally speaking, when ordering takeout, there will be a certain extra cost, such as delivery and service fees. And there is also the risk of food safety. After all, the supervision of the quality of takeout is imperfect. So when ordering takeout, it's important to remember to verify the food safety of the store.

Summing up, although ordering takeout is much more convenient than cooking at home, some attention should be paid to food safety. Only in this way, can we enjoy the delicious food relievedly.

译文：外卖

如今，点外卖已经成为人们生活中不可或缺的一部分。它不仅可以节省我们大量的做饭时间，还可以在饮食结构方面给我们更多的自由和选择。随着外卖订单的增加，不少外卖送餐平台相继出现。点外卖远比在家做饭方便。

说起外卖的好处，首先是节省时间。如今，人们变得更加忙碌，家庭聚餐的时间变得非常宝贵。此外，有些人晚上加班，没有时间做饭。因此，外卖不仅解决了需要解决的晚餐问题，还减少了自己做饭的时间。而且点外卖也很方便。你可以省去外出购买食材和烹饪的麻烦。你可以通过互联网点外卖，在家也可以吃到美味的食物。

点外卖也可以根据饮食结构为人们提供更多选择。谈到食物，每个人都有不同的口味偏好。有些人喜欢火锅，有些人喜欢寿司。通过点外卖，每个人都可以满足自己的口味。如果你想吃什么，可以直接点外卖。另外，当谈到食物的种类时，点外卖的食物品类也比自己做的饭更丰富。

当然，外卖也有一些缺点。一般来说，点外卖会产生一定的额外费用，比如配送费和服务费。外卖也会存在食品安全风险。毕竟，对外卖品质的监管是不完善的。因此，在点外卖时，记得核实店铺的食品安全性。

综上所述，尽管点外卖比在家做饭方便得多，但仍应注意食品安全。只有这样，我们才能安心地享用美食。

Part 5 Exercises

Task 1 Match China's eight major cuisines on the left with their characteristics on the right. Then discuss with you partner which cuisine do you like best and why.

1. Shandong cuisine	A. thick and pungent flavor
2. Guangdong cuisine	B. saltiness and umami
3. Sichuan cuisine	C. freshness, tenderness, softness and smoothness
4. Jiangsu cuisine	D. sweet, sour, salty and savory
5. Zhejiang cuisine	E. heavy and a little salty
6. Fujian cuisine	F. light
7. Hunan cuisine	G. strong and hot taste
8. Anhui cuisine	H. slightly sweet

Task 2 Translate the following English dish names into Chinese according to Dialogue 2.

1. Mapo Tofu ____________________
2. Twice Cooked Pork ____________________
3. Kung Pao Chicken ______________________
4. Sliced Beef and Ox Tongue in Chilli Sauce ______________________

Task 3 Complete the following dialogue according to Dialogue 3.

Hostess: Welcome. May I help you?

Diner: Yes, I have a 1.___________ (预订) for tonight.

Hostess: 2. ___________ what name did you make your reservation, please?

Diner: It was under Ms. Smith.

Hostess: Yes, Ms. Smith. Three people in your party, right?

Diner: That's right.

Hostess: Your table is ready. This way, please.

Diner: Here's the 3.____________ (菜单). Our waitress will be with you in a few minutes.

(Several minutes later)

Waitress: Good evening. May I take your 4.___________ (点菜) now?

Diner: Yes. Please give us three Sirloin Steaks. We all want set meals.

Waitress: And how would you like your steaks, rare, medium, or well-done?

Diner: All well-done, please.

Waitress: Right away, Madam.

(Two hours later, at the cashier counter)

Diner: Split the bill, please. We'd like to go 5.___________ (AA 制 / 各付各的账).

Hostess: Of course. How would you like to pay for the 6.___________ (账单)?

Diner: By WeChat.

Task 4 Role Play

Student A: Imagine you are a guest in a Chinese restaurant.

Ask questions about the specialties of the restaurant and order food and drinks.

Student B: Imagine you are a waiter in the Chinese restaurant.

Answer the guest's questions and recommend some specialties.

Change roles and try the role play again.

Unit 4

Part 6 Self-evaluation

评价项目	评价内容	自我诊断	改进措施
语言知识	I learn many common words and expressions about food.	☐ Identifying ☐ Understanding ☐ Mastering	
认知能力	I know how to make a reservation and order at a restaurant.	☐ Distinction ☐ Merit ☐ Pass ☐ Fail	
沟通能力	I can order and check out at both a Chinese restaurant and a Western restaurant.	☐ Distinction ☐ Merit ☐ Pass ☐ Fail	
文化意识	I get to learn that traditional Chinese food is popular with more and more people.	☐ Increasing ☐ Developing ☐ Weakening	

Part 7 Culture

Traditional Chinese Food and Culture Draw Throngs of New Yorkers

(from *https://www.chinadaily.com.cn*, Updated: 2023-07-01)

A Chinese food and culture festival won New Yorkers' hearts and stomachs on June 24 with its debut on a section of street at Washington Square Park in Lower Manhattan.

The festival showcased authentic Chinese food like soup dumplings, dandan noodles, kebabs, pastries, flower cakes, bingtang hulu (sugarcoated hawthorn), jianbing (a savory pancake), sugar paintings, stinky tofu and others from around 35 vendors.

Foodies waited in long lines at some popular stands and the waiting time for the jianbing event exceeded two hours.

Summer showers didn't dampen New Yorkers' enthusiasm and the street remained crowded throughout the afternoon.

More than 30,000 people joined the free event from 10 am to 6 pm last Saturday, according to Xu Xuan, founder of the festival, which is branded as Dragon Fest.

Food is the best starting point for people to understand and appreciate Chinese culture, Xu said.

Vendors from Qingmu Dessert Lab offered Chinese pastries and wore traditional Chinese clothing known as hanfu.

A set of four pastries was made to represent the four seasons with ingredients collected throughout the year, according to an associate with Qingmu Dessert Lab.

Jianbing, a popular street food in North China, drew many people's interest as its vendor Gem Bing Shop is nearby.

New Yorkers could also taste flower cake with ingredients imported from Southwest China's Yunnan province.

Meanwhile, staff members from the restaurant brand Mala Project were busy fulfilling orders for spicy dry pot, representing neo-Sichuan cuisine.

The presence of Seattle-based frozen dumpling service MiLa at the festival illustrates the popularity of authentic Chinese food in the US market. Its participation in the festival also marks the first largescale promotion of the brand in New York.

Founded in 2018, MiLa switched to online sales of frozen soup dumplings after the start of the COVID-19 pandemic. It then shipped products to customers across the United States as its popularity increased, said Zhang Xiaohan, brand marketing and partnership lead with MiLa.

Zhang sees enormous potential for authentic Chinese food in the mainstream market. MiLa started to supply Costco Wholesale stores on the West Coast in June.

Chinese cuisine is not merely fried dumplings, steamed buns or chow mein (fried noodles), nor does it mean American-style Chinese food, said Xu, the event's founder.

Xu said that she mulled over organizing such a festival as early as 2019 to present people with a one-stop experience of Chinese food.

Moreover, people can also try bubble tea, Sichuan-style spicy chili fried chicken, fried skewers, egg waffles, Mochi ice cream and others.

The festival is expected to be held at three other locations in Manhattan in August and September.

Unit 5

Friends and Families

扫码看

Learning Objectives

After learning this unit, you should be able to:

1. get familiar with the words and expressions concerning friends and families;
2. know how to talk about families and friends;
3. know that filial piety is a cultural trait.

Unit 5

Part 1 Topic Words and Expressions

扫码听

Family Visit
- campus
- restaurant
- museum
- aunt
- uncle
- cousin
- apartment
- bathroom
- guest

Talking about Friends
- winter vacation
- dine
- curly
- shoulder-length
- neatly
- fashionably
- deal with
- abate
- misery
- grief

Li Hua's Family
- couple
- common
- independent
- maintain
- separately
- freedom
- personal
- appropriate
- relieve

Three-child Policy
- shift
- census
- populous
- annul
- impose
- halt
- explosion
- optimize
- preserve
- inclusive
- complementary
- integrate

Part 2 Lead-in

Li Hua and Jack talk about their families. On winter vacation. Wang Xia talks with her high school classmate, Li Li, about her new friends in college.

Part 3 Dialogs

Dialog 1 Family Visit

扫码听

(Li Hua and Jack meet on campus. They are talking about their families.)

Li Hua: Good morning, Jack. How are you doing?

Jack: I'm fine, Li Hua. But I'm tired.

Li Hua: Why are you tired?

Jack: My parents and grandparents are visiting me this week. I am very busy.

Li Hua: Are you taking them to many places?

Jack: Yes. We're going to restaurants, movies and museums.

Li Hua: How long are they staying?

Jack: They are staying until this Saturday.

Li Hua: My family visits sometimes. I take them to many places, too. I've heard you Americans usually have a big family. So how many members are there in your family?

Jack: There are six people in my family, my father, my mother, my brother, my two sisters and I.

Li Hua: Oh, that's a large family.

Jack: My mother has three brothers and four sisters. And my father has two brothers and two sisters.

Li Hua: So you have lots of aunts and uncles?

Jack: I do. And sometimes they all visit my family at the same time!

Li Hua: Then you're really busy!

Jack: Yes. Busy but happy. I have a lot of cousins, too.

Li Hua: Do they ever stay with you?

Jack: Some of them do. But my apartment isn't so roomy. And I only have one bathroom!

Li Hua: That's a problem for guests.

Jack: So I hope I can have a big house in the future.

Li Hua: May your dream come true.

Jack: Thank you.

Notes

1. I've heard you Americans usually have a big family.
   我听说美国人通常家里人口很多。
2. How many members are there in your family?
   你家有几口人？
3. May your dream come true.
   愿你梦想成真。

Dialog 2 Li Hua's Family

扫码听

(Jack asks Li Hua about his family.)

Jack: Li Hua, how many people are there in your family?

Li Hua: Three. I'm the only child of my parents.

Jack: The only child?

Li Hua: Yes. Couples in my parents' age usually have one child.

Jack: In America, some couples usually have more than one child and they like to have a big family.

Li Hua: Well, many Chinese also have a large family, for it is common that three generations live under one roof. I heard that Americans prefer to live apart from their parents when they grow up. Is it true?

Jack: Yes, it's true. We enjoy an independent life. But we often make phone calls to each other and arrange a family reunion at Christmas, Thanksgiving or something like that.

Li Hua: I think it's great to be able to maintain independence and keep in touch with families at the same time. You know Chinese families are also changing.

Jack: What's the change?

Li Hua: More and more Chinese people choose to live separately from their adult children when they grow old so that they can enjoy more freedom and personal space.

Jack: That's great. I think family members should maintain appropriate distance. I wonder if Chinese couples in this age usually have one child, too.

Li Hua: It depends. Now our country not only encourages families to have a second child, but also encourages them to have a third one.

Jack: Really?

Li Hua: Yes. Our government does this to relieve the pressure of the aging of the population and improve China's population structure.

Jack: Anyway, that's a good thing.

Li Hua: I think so.

Notes

1. I'm the only child of my parents.

   我是独生子。

2. It is common that three generations live under one roof.

   三代同堂是很常见的。

3. It's great to be able to maintain independence and keep in touch with families at the same time.

   能够保持独立，同时又能和家人保持联系，真是太棒了。

Dialog 3 Talking about Friends

扫码听

(On winter vacation, Wang Xia meets her best friend from high school, Li Li. They are talking about their new friends in college.)

Li Li: Hi, Wang Xia. Long time no see. I miss you so much.

Wang Xia: Hello, Li Li. We haven't seen each other for a whole semester. I miss you, too.

Li Li: How's your college life?

Wang Xia: Wonderful. I enjoy it.

Li Li: How are you getting on with your roommates?

Wang Xia: I get on really well with them. We have a lot in common, so we often do things together, such as dining in the canteen, running on the playground, reading in the library and so on.

Li Li: How lucky you are! Besides your lovely roommates, have you made any other friends?

Wang Xia: Yes, of course. I do have a special close friend in college.

Li Li: Come on. I'm all ears.

Wang Xia: Her name is Li Na. She has the same family name as you.

Li Li: What does she look like?

Wang Xia: She is tall and slim. She has big eyes and curly shoulder-length hair. She is always dressed neatly and fashionably.

Li Li: She must be a pretty girl.

Wang Xia: Yes, she is. What's more, she is kind, helpful and smart. She is always ready to help. She is not afraid of dangers and difficulties. She always come up with good plans when others have no ideas.

Li Li: After hearing what you said, I also like her.

Wang Xia: I believe you will be good friends with her if you meet her. I can share my joy with her and she always care about me when I am in bad mood.

Li Li: So everyone needs friends, for there are a lot of things that we can't deal with only by ourselves, but friends just make up for it.

Wang Xia: When we are down, our friends lift us up. When we lose our ways, our friends guide us and cheer us on.

Li Li: Just as it is said that friendship improves happiness and abates misery by doubling our joy and dividing our grief.

Wang Xia: I can't agree with you anymore.

Unit 5

Notes

1. How are you getting on with your roommates?
   你和室友相处得怎么样？

2. When we are down, our friends lift us up. When we lose our ways, our friends guide us and cheer us on.
   当我们情绪低落时，朋友会鼓舞我们。当我们迷失方向时，朋友会引导我们，为我们加油。
3. Friendship improves happiness and abates misery by doubling our joy and dividing our grief.
   友谊使我们的快乐加倍，使我们的悲伤减半，从而增进幸福，减轻痛苦。

Part 4 Passage

Three-child Policy

China has officially further relaxed its family planning policy, supporting couples that wish to have a third child. It was decided at a meeting of the Political Bureau of Communist Party of China (CPC) Central Committee.

The policy shift came not long after China's once-in-a-decade census, data from which showed a decline in births in the world's most populous country. Per the census, Chinese population grew at its slowest rate during the last decade since the 1950s.

In 2016, China annulled the one-child policy, which had been imposed to halt a population explosion in 1982, replacing it with a two-child limit. It was acknowledged at the meeting that despite the two-child policy achieving positive results, the aging of the population in China has deepened in recent years.

Thus, it was determined that further optimizing the childbirth policy and implementing the policy to allow couples to have three children with supportive measures will help improve China's population structure, relieve the pressure of the aging population and preserve the country's human resource advantages.

The key difference between the two-child limit, which failed to reverse China's birth rate due to the high cost of raising children for urban couples, and the new third-child policy is that the government now pays more attention to support couples to have more kids and the new childbirth rate policy will come along with inclusive supportive measures, says Wei Nanzhi, research fellow from Institute of American Studies, Chinese Academy of Social Science.

At the meeting it was decided that all levels of government should implement complementary policies in supporting families that follow the new childbirth policy, with integrated consideration in marriage, childbirth, parenting and education.

译文：三孩政策

中共中央政治局会议决定，中国正式进一步放宽计划生育政策，支持希望生育第三个孩子的夫妻。

该政策的转变发生在中国十年一次的人口普查之后不久。人口普查数据显示，作为全球人口最多的国家，中国的人口出生率正在下降，中国近十年的人口增长速度降至自20世纪50年代以来的最低水平。

2016年，中国取消了1982年为遏制人口爆发式增长而实施的独生子女政策，取而代之的是二孩政策。会议承认，尽管二孩政策取得了积极成果，

Unit 5

但近年来中国人口老龄化状况仍有所加剧。

因此，进一步优化生育政策，实施一对夫妻生育三个孩子的扶持措施，将有利于改善中国的人口结构，有利于缓解人口老龄化压力，保持我国人力资源禀赋优势。

中国社会科学院美国研究所研究员魏南志表示，由于城市里抚养孩子成本高昂，二孩政策未能扭转中国出生率下降的趋势，新的三孩政策意味着生育政策将更加注重支持多生孩子的夫妻——新的生育政策将伴随着包容性的支持措施。

会议决定，各级政府要对实行新生育政策的家庭实施配套扶持政策，统筹兼顾婚姻、生育、育儿和教育等方面。

Part 5 Exercises

Task 1 Pair work. Complete the chart.

Male	Female	Male	Female
father	mother	brother	sister
son	1.__________	2.__________	aunt
grandfather	grandmother	grandson	granddaughter
3.__________	niece	cousin	cousin
4.__________	mother-in-law	brother-in-law	5.__________
husband	6.__________	7.__________	bride

Task 2 Translate the English expressions of family members into Chinese.

1. bride ____________
2. bridegroom ____________
3. elder brother ____________
4. younger sister ____________
5. brother-in-law ____________
6. mother-in-law ____________
7. nephew ____________
8. niece ____________
9. siblings ____________
10. grandparents ____________

Task 3 Translate the following quotes about friendship into Chinese.

1. A friend in need is a friend indeed. ____________
2. A life without a friend is a life without a sun. ____________
3. A father is a treasure, a brother is a comfort, but a friend is both. ____________
4. Friends must part. ____________
5. A good book is the best of friends, the same today and forever. ____________

Task 4 Role Play

Student A: Imagine you are a foreign student.

Ask questions about the differences of the titles of family members between China and the West.

Student B: Imagine you are the friend of A.

Answer A's questions about the titles of Chinese family members.

Change roles and try the role play again.

Unit 5

Part 6 Self-evaluation

评价项目	评价内容	自我诊断	改进措施
语言知识	I learn many common words and expressions about friends and families.	☐ Identifying ☐ Understanding ☐ Mastering	
认知能力	I know how to talk about friends and families.	☐ Distinction ☐ Merit ☐ Pass ☐ Fail	
沟通能力	I can describe friends and family members in English.	☐ Distinction ☐ Merit ☐ Pass ☐ Fail	
文化意识	I get to learn about Chinese filial piety culture.	☐ Increasing ☐ Developing ☐ Weakening	

Part 7 Culture

Filial Piety Does Not Need a Code (Excerpt)

(from *https://www.chinadaily.com.cn*, Updated: 2012-08-31)

Almost all Chinese will agree that filial piety is a cultural trait that should be adhered to, and the old saying, "filial piety is the first among 100 virtues", will be never out of date in Chinese society. Then why has the new code of conduct for filial piety issued by the office of the National Committee for senior citizen affairs created a controversy?

Adult children, according to the code of conduct, are required to do 24 things for their parents in their daily life. By recommending these everyday actions, the authorities paint a vivid picture of a caring middle class family: Adult children are emotionally close to their parents and satisfy their economic and emotional needs by supporting them financially, visiting them frequently and spending more leisure time with them. This is a wonderful picture of a really harmonious family and most of us long for it. But a majority of Chinese would say: "Are we all part of this wonderful picture?"

Unit 5

Responding to an online survey conducted by a newspaper and a website in Henan province, only 16.9 percent people said they met the basic requirements of the code. It would mean that more than 80 percent of the respondents don't (or don't want to) take care of their elderly parents. But we know that is not true. Experience tells us that lack of money and time prevents most of the people from meeting the requirements of the filial code of conduct.

Unit 6

Health

扫码看

Learning Objectives

After learning this unit, you should be able to:

1. get familiar with the words and expressions concerning health;
2. introduce the procedures of seeing a doctor in English;
3. know that Chinese public medical treatment has been greatly developed.

Unit 6

Part 1 Topic Words and Expressions

扫码听

Feeling Sick

- throat
- sore
- look run down
- thermometer
- temperature
- armpit
- degree
- ibuprofen
- urgently
- participate in
- volunteer
- influenza
- infect
- under the weather

At the Hospital

- traditional Chinese medicine (TCM)
- appointment
- official account
- designated area
- generate
- registration
- consultation room
- tonsillitis
- inflame
- appetite
- pulse
- prescription
- patent medicine
- herbal medicine
- pharmacy
- instruction

Keeping Healthy

- tonsils
- recover
- dieting
- resistance
- efficient
- centralized
- suggestion
- kind of
- pound

Know What a Balanced Diet Is

- protein
- carbohydrate
- vitamin
- mineral
- nutrient
- fiber
- starch
- energize

Part 2 Lead-in

Wang Xia plans to take part in a volunteer activity this weekend. But she is sick on Saturday morning and have to ask for leave to see a doctor. After resting for several days, she returns to the college and decides to take exercise together with Li Hua.

Part 3 Dialogs

Dialog 1 Feeling Sick

扫码听

(Mum comes to wake up Wang Xia on Saturday morning.)

Mum: Wake up, honey. Your alarm clock has been ringing twice! It's time to get up!

Wang Xia: Er... I know, mum, but I'm not feeling very well now.

Mum: What's wrong with you?

Wang Xia: My head hurts a lot and my throat is sore.

Mum: Well, let me see... Poor girl, you really look run down.

Wang Xia: Yes, mum, I feel a little bit sick.

Mum: Oh, it's a bit hot on your forehead. I need to take a thermometer for you.

(Mum comes back with a clinic thermometer.)

Mum: Now Let me measure your temperature at first. Put this thermometer under your armpit, honey.

Wang Xia: OK, mum.

(A few minutes later)

Mum: Sweetheart, it's about time. Now take out the thermometer and show it to me.

Wang Xia: Okay, here you are.

Mum: Oh my, your temperature is 38.5 degrees!

Wang Xia: Really? No wonder I find it a little cold right now.

Mum: Well, I'm afraid some ibuprofen and a sound sleep are urgent for you.

Wang Xia: But I have to participate in the volunteer activity today.

Mum: All you need now is a good, long rest. Anyway, if it is the influenza, it will infect others. I suggest you take a sick leave.

Wang Xia: Maybe you are right, mum. I'll call for a leave.

Mum: That's a good idea. Just wait a second, I'll get the medicine for you. Take the medicine and you'll be fine after a good sleep.

Wang Xia: What if I'm still under the weather?

Mum: Don't worry, my girl. If you can't get over it, I'll drive you to the hospital to see a doctor.

Wang Xia: Thanks, mum.

Notes

1. You really look run down.
   你看起来挺憔悴的。
2. Put this thermometer under your armpit.
   把体温计夹到腋下。
3. What if I'm still under the weather?
   如果我还是不舒服呢？

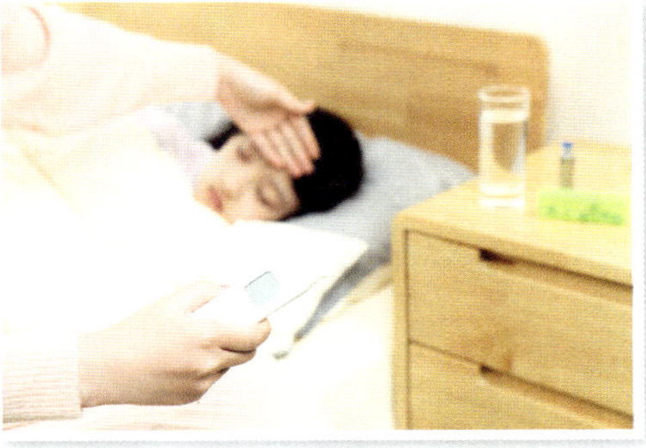

Dialog 2 At the Hospital

(Mum drives Wang Xia to the hospital and Wang Xia is in the waiting hall now.)

扫码听

Nurse: Good afternoon. What can I do for you?

Wang Xia: Good afternoon. I have a fever and I want to see a traditional Chinese medicine doctor.

Nurse: So, have you ever made an appointment?

Wang Xia: Yes, I have already booked on your official account online.

Nurse: OK, then please place your ID card on the designated area of the machine to sign in according to the tips on the screen.

Wang Xia: Oh my god! I forgot to bring my ID card!

Nurse: Well, take it easy. The machine can also scan the QR code generated in your appointment registration to help you sign in. Can you find it?

Wang Xia: Let me have a try. Mm... Is it this QR code?

Nurse: Yes, that's it. Please put the code over here. OK, now your sign-in is completed. Please wait a moment. When your number is called out, you can enter the consultation room.

Wang Xia: Thank you very much!

(Wang Xia is in the consultation room.)

Doctor: Sit down, please. What's the matter with you?

Wang Xia: I have a terrible headache, doctor, and a sore throat. I am running a fever, too.

Doctor: How long have you been like that?

Wang Xia: About a day.

Doctor: Well, let me have a look at your throat first. Please open your mouth and say "ah".

Wang Xia: Ah...

Doctor: OK, show me your tongue... Good. Don't be nervous. You have slight tonsillitis and it makes your throat inflamed. How is your appetite?

Wang Xia: Er... Not so good.

Doctor: I see. What about your temperature? Have you taken it?

Wang Xia: Yes, it was 38.5 in the morning and reduced to 38 after I took some ibuprofen.

Doctor: Now, let me feel your pulse.

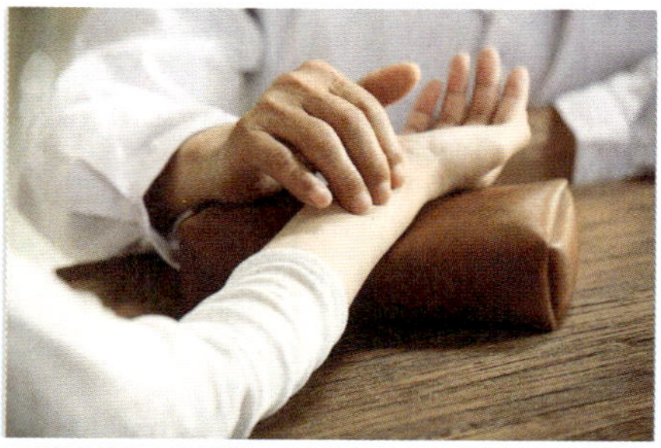

(After a while)

Doctor: En... Your pulse is weak.

Wang Xia: Is it serious?

Doctor: Not too serious, but you'd better be patient. It'll take you some time to recover.

Wang Xia: So, is there any useful treatment you can offer?

Doctor: Well, yes, I'll write you a prescription. Would you like some Chinese patent medicine or herbal medicine?

Wang Xia: I'd like to try herbal medicine, please. It is said that it really works.

Doctor: All right. Now please go to the pharmacy to get this prescription filled and take the medicine according to the instructions. You'll be better soon.

Wang Xia: Thank you, doctor. Bye.

Notes

1. I have already booked on your official account online.

   我已经在你们公众号上预约了。

2. Please place your ID card on the designated area of the machine to sign in according to the tips on the screen.

   请按照屏幕上的提示将您的身份证放到机器指定区域进行签到。

3. You have slight tonsillitis and it makes your throat inflamed.

   你的扁桃体有点发炎，导致喉咙也发炎了。

4. Please go to the pharmacy to get this prescription filled and take the medicine according to the instructions.

   请到药房照方抓药，并按说明服用。

Dialog 3 Keeping Healthy

扫码听

(Wang Xia meets Li Hua on the campus.)

Li Hua: Hi, Wang Xia, Long time no see.

Wang Xia: Hi, Li Hua.

Li Hua: I heard you took several days off. What happened?

Unit 6

Wang Xia: Er... I took a sick leave. My tonsils were inflamed last Saturday.

Li Hua: Oh, it must have been a hard time for you. Do you feel better right now?

Wang Xia: Well, I've almost recovered. Li Hua, can I ask you something? I want your opinions.

Li Hua: OK, go ahead.

Wang Xia: Do you think dieting for weight loss is bad for health?

Li Hua: Yes, of course. Why?

Wang Xia: Recently, I felt I was gaining weight and went on a diet. But my mum thought this was the reason why my resistance became weaker, which made me sick easily.

Li Hua: I'm on your mother's side.

Wang Xia: Why? Everyone does it this way. It's efficient!

Li Hua: But not healthy, you know. You need to take a balanced diet to keep fit.

Wang Xia: Well, maybe you are right. I don't want to get out of control of my weight.

Li Hua: Why don't you join our fitness club? We have professional training to help members to get fit.

Wang Xia: That sounds cool. When are your club activities?

Li Hua: We usually have centralized activities on Thursday afternoons and group activities almost every afternoon. Today happens to be Thursday. So, do you want to go then?

Wang Xia: Yeah, that sounds great. Thanks for your suggestions!

Li Hua: My pleasure. Honestly, I kind of want to lose a few pounds, too.

Wang Xia: Then let's make sure we stay on task. Doing this together should make it easier, right?

Li Hua: Yes, that's what I'm thinking. Let's meet at the gate of the sports field at 2:00 this afternoon.

Wang Xia: Alright, I'll see you there.

Notes

1. I heard you took several days off.
   我听说你请了几天假。
2. I'm on your mother's side.
   我同意你母亲的观点。
3. You need to take a balanced diet to keep fit.
   你需要采取均衡的饮食来保持健康。

Part 4 Passage

Know What a Balanced Diet Is

Eating a healthy diet means you're getting the balance of proteins, fats, and carbohydrates, along with the vitamins and minerals your body needs to function well. To get all of these nutrients, you need to make sure you eat a variety of foods and your meals contain some carbohydrates, proteins, fats, and fibers at each meal.

A good rule of thumb for eating a well-balanced meal is to consume about 1 or 2 servings of vegetables or fruits per meal, along with a serving of fats, starch (such as whole grain, legumes, or starchy vegetables) and some proteins (legumes, tofu, chicken, fish, eggs, yogurt, etc).

For example, you may have 1 cup of low-fat yogurt with 3/4 cup of blueberries, 1 tablespoon of chopped nuts and a handful of whole grain cereal for breakfast. Or you might eat 2 slices of whole grain toast with 1/3 avocado, lettuce, sliced tomatoes, and chopped eggs. This will make you full and energized.

A common mistake is not eating enough fruits and vegetables or high-fiber foods. Another pitfall is eating too much fried foods and sugary snacks and sodas (or any foods that supply a lot of calories without enough nutrients).

译文：了解均衡饮食

健康饮食意味着你获取的蛋白质、脂肪、碳水化合物以及你身体运作所需的维生素和矿物质之间要达到均衡。要获取所有这些营养元素，你得确保你摄入的食物种类足够丰富，而且每餐都含有一些碳水化合物、蛋白质、脂肪和纤维。

检验一餐是否营养均衡的标准是，每餐要吃大约一到两份蔬菜或水果，再加上一份脂肪、一份淀粉（如全谷物、豆类或淀粉类蔬菜）和一份蛋白质（豆类、豆腐、鸡肉、鱼肉、鸡蛋、酸奶等）。

例如，早餐时，你可以选择一杯低脂酸奶，加上 3/4 杯蓝莓、一汤匙切碎的坚果和一把全麦谷物。或者，你可以吃两片全麦烤面包，配上 1/3 个牛油果、生菜、切片西红柿和切碎的鸡蛋。这会让你有饱腹感并充满活力。

人们常犯的一个错误是，水果、蔬菜或高纤维食物摄入不足；而另一个误区则是油炸食品、含糖的零食和碳酸饮料（或任何热量高但营养成分低的食物）摄入过多。

Part 5 Exercises

Task 1 Please write the names of the following symptoms in English.

1. ______________________________

2. ______________________________

3. ______________________________

4. ______________________________

5. ______________________________

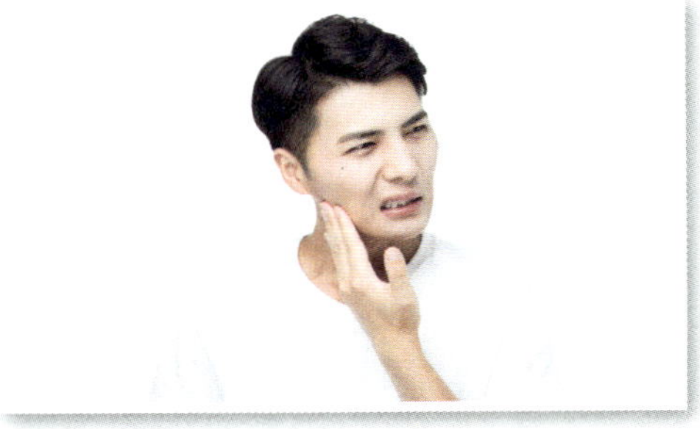

6. ______________________________

Task 2 Tom is sick. He wants to make an appointment online to see a doctor. Please help him to put the following steps in the correct order.

A. Open your WeChat, enter the hospital's official account, and click on the bottom of the "Smart Hospital".

B. On the skipped page, select "Special Clinic", which generally does not require a special disease clinic.

C. On the doctor's homepage, you can choose morning or afternoon appointments. If it shows "full", you cannot book any more, if not, then select "click to book".

D. If you need to book an appointment with Traditional Chinese Medicine, select "Traditional Chinese Medicine Department" on the left side of the list, then click on "Traditional Chinese Medicine Clinic" in the list.

E. In the popup list box, choose "Appointment Registration". (note that you usually need to book a few days in advance, otherwise, you may not be able to book.)

F. On the popup window, choose the specific time for that day, and the appointment is completed. After completing the appointment, be sure to pay the registration fee before the scheduled time.

G. On the skipped page again, choose the specific time for the appointment, such as Sunday, and then choose the specific doctor to see in the list below.

________→________→________→________→________→________→________

Task 3 Wang Xia has joined the fitness club. She needs to choose a fitness program to work out. Please help her to make a choice and tell her your reasons.

1. ______________________________

2. ______________________________

3. ______________________

4. ______________________

5. ______________________

6. ______________________

Task 4 Role Play

Student A: Imagine you are a doctor in the hospital.

Ask questions about your patient and make your diagnosis.

Student B: Imagine you have a stomachache and come to see a doctor.

Answer the doctor's questions and ask for proper treatment.

Change roles and try the role play again.

Unit 6

Part 6 Self-evaluation

评价项目	评价内容	自我诊断	改进措施
语言知识	I learn many useful words and expressions about health.	☐ Identifying ☐ Understanding ☐ Mastering	
认知能力	I know how to make an appointment online.	☐ Distinction ☐ Merit ☐ Pass ☐ Fail	
沟通能力	I can introduce the common symptoms in English.	☐ Distinction ☐ Merit ☐ Pass ☐ Fail	
文化意识	I get to learn about great achievements in Chinese medical treatment.	☐ Increasing ☐ Developing ☐ Weakening	

Part 7 Culture

TCM study identifies compounds in COVID drug

(from *https://www.chinadaily.com.cn*, Updated: 2023-04-26)

Researchers have successfully identified key antiviral and bioactive anti-inflammatory compounds in a traditional Chinese medicine therapy widely used to treat COVID-19. The findings are expected to shed light on the way TCM works against the virus, and to help promote global acceptance of TCM.

Researchers discovered six compounds with notable antiviral effects and five components with obvious anti-inflammatory effects in a decoction known as Huashi Paidu, according to a study written by researchers from Academy of Chinese Medical Sciences and other institutions.

Four of the compounds exhibited both antiviral and anti-inflammatory effects, according to the article, which was published on Monday in The Proceedings of the National Academy of Sciences, a peer reviewed journal.

The decoction, which is made of raw ephedra, almond, raw rhubarb, licorice and a number of medicinal herbs, has shown effectiveness in easing COVID-19 symptoms.

It is one of six TCM therapies recommended by top Chinese health authorities to treat the virus.

Xu Haiyu, a researcher from Academy of Chinese Medical Sciences' Institute of Chinese Materia Medica, told Xinhua News Agency that the synergistic effect of multicomponents and multitargets might be the reason TCM therapies like Huashi Baidu are effective in relieving COVID-19 symptoms.

He added that the findings provide a template for explaining the way TCM works and support future research into the development of TCM drugs.

Unit 7

Public Transport

扫码看

Learning Objectives

After learning this unit, you should be able to:

1. get familiar with the words and expressions concerning public transport;
2. introduce the procedures of taking the airplane, the high-speed train and the subway in English;
3. know that Chinese public transport has been greatly developed and ranked among the top in the world.

Unit 7

Part 1 Topic Words and Expressions

扫码听

At the Airport

- check in
- take off
- flight number
- aisle seat
- window seat
- conveyor belt
- luggage bill
- boarding pass
- carry-on luggage
- security check
- electronic device

Taking the Subway

- take the subway
- subway station
- sign
- easy access
- rail transit
- automated ticket machine
- push the button
- fare
- pay in cash
- scan code

Booking Train Tickets

- high-speed train
- rail station
- departure
- log on/in
- destination station
- inquiry
- ticket price
- business-class seat
- first-class seat
- second-class seat

Captain's Announcements

- captain
- overhead bin
- cabin attendant
- flight attendant
- fasten seat belt
- tray table
- cruise
- time of arrival
- power off
- disembark
- checked baggage
- terminal building

Part 2 Lead-in

Li Hua and Wang Xia are two freshmen of a vocational college. They are going to visit Suzhou, where a skill contest will be held. They plan to fly to Shanghai, then take a high-speed train to Suzhou and finally take the subway to the local hotel.

Part 3 Dialogs

Dialog 1 At the Airport

(At the Daxing International Airport, Li Hua and Wang Xia are to take a flight to Shanghai.)

扫码听

Li Hua: I'm too excited because this is my first time to take a flight!

Wang Xia: Though we have booked the air tickets online in advance, passengers are to check in at the airport an hour and a half before the plane takes off.

Li Hua: Where is our check-in counter?

Wang Xia: We can find the check-in counter according to the flight number on the ticket.

Li Hua: Oh, that's check-in counter 12. Down that way on your left.

Wang Xia: OK. Let's go!

(They are at the check-in counter.)

Unit 7

Wang Xia: I would like to check in, please.

Clerk: May I have your ID card, please?

Wang Xia: Sure, here you are.

Clerk: Would you like to sit at the window or the aisle?

Wang Xia: I would like an aisle seat, please.

Clerk: How many pieces of luggage will you check in?

Wang Xia: Just one suitcase.

Clerk: Please place it on the conveyor belt.

Wang Xia: OK.

Clerk: Here are your luggage bill and your boarding pass.

Wang Xia: Thank you.

Clerk: (Waving to the next in line) May I see your ID card, please?

Li Hua: Here. And I would like a window seat.

Clerk: OK. Anything to check?

Li Hua: I have only one backpack.

Clerk: Sir, you can keep that backpack as carry-on luggage.

Li Hua: OK, great.

Clerk: Sir, here is your boarding pass. Please go to security check.

(Li Hua and Wang Xia go to security check and wait in line.)

Security officer: ID card (passport) and boarding pass please. Please take out any liquids, loose items, and electronic devices. Remove your coat, jacket and put your bags in a tray.

Li Hua: I have a bottle of water.

Security officer: I'm sorry, sir. No liquids are permitted to be taken. Tight regulations, either drink it or dispose of it.

Li Hua: OK. I'll drink it.

Security officer: Please put all carry-on luggage in this basket and then place it on the conveyor.

Wang Xia: OK.

Security officer: Sir, you are good to go.

Li Hua: We got through security. Can we board the plane?

Wang Xia: Yes! Our flight leaves from Gate B16 and boarding begins at 10:00 a.m. Let's go!

Notes

1. Though we have booked the air tickets online in advance, passengers are to check in at the airport an hour and a half before the plane takes off.
   虽然我们已经提前在网上预订了机票，但乘客们必须在飞机起飞前一个半小时到机场办理登机手续。
2. Here are your luggage bill and your boarding pass.
   这是您的行李单和登机牌。
3. Please take out any liquids, loose items, and electronic devices.
   请取出液体、零散物品和电子设备。

Dialog 2 Booking Train Tickets

扫码听

(Before arriving in Shanghai, Li Hua and Wang Xia are talking about booking high-speed train tickets.)

Li Hua: We need to book high-speed train tickets from Shanghai to Suzhou in advance.

Wang Xia: Good idea! So we can go directly to the high-speed rail station and take the train to Suzhou from the airport when we arrive.

Li Hua: But I haven't tried to book a train ticket myself.

Wang Xia: It's easy. Let me show you.

Li Hua: Great!

Wang Xia: There are several ways to book train tickets in advance, such as booking tickets at a train station or at a ticket office. But the most convenient way is to book at China Railway's official website *www.12306.cn*, which sells tickets 15 days before departure.

Li Hua: I've heard about this website. Can it be operated on a mobile phone? It's much easier to use a mobile App.

Wang Xia: Of course it can. First download 12306 China Railway mobile App and log on. Enter the departure and destination stations on the home page, select the travel date and then click the button of "Ticket Inquiry".

Li Hua: OK. I find another option, "Student Ticket", below the date. I can also click it, right?

Wang Xia: Sure, so you can get a discount. Next, click on the high-speed train number you want to book and enter the next page.

Li Hua: Wow, I see here are different seats and corresponding ticket prices.

Wang Xia: Yes, you can choose business-class seat, first-class seat and second-class seat.

Li Hua: I guess most people will select the second-class seats, as they're the cheapest.

Wang Xia: Yes. Then you can click the button below to choose the passenger.

Li Hua: This is the first time for me to use this mobile App, so I need to add the passenger information, right?

Wang Xia: Yeah, that's it. And you can select your seat.

Li Hua: Awesome! I'll choose a window seat.

Wang Xia: Then you can submit the order and pay it immediately.

Li Hua: Wow, I manage to book a high-speed train ticket myself. The App is so convenient and efficient!

Notes

1. But the most convenient way is to book at China Railway's official website *www.12306.cn*, which sells tickets 15 days before departure.

   但最方便的方式是在中国铁路官方网站 www.12306.cn 订票，该网站预售期为发车前 15 天。

2. First download 12306 China Railway mobile App and log on.

   首先，下载 12306 中国铁路移动应用程序，并登录。

3. Enter the departure and destination stations on the home page, select the travel date and then click the button of "Ticket Inquiry".

   在首页输入出发地和目的地站点，选择出行日期，点击"查询车票"按键。

Dialog 3 Taking the Subway

扫码听

(Li Hua and Wang Xia are at the Suzhou Railway Station. They will go to the hotel.)

Li Hua: This is the Suzhou Railway Station. How classic and elegant it is!

Wang Xia: Yes, and it's also very advanced. Next we're going to our hotel. I guess the fastest way is to take the subway.

Li Hua: Is there a subway station near here?

Wang Xia: Of course! Let's take a look at the various signs posted nearby, which will show us the way.

Li Hua: Look! There is a sign hanging in front.

Wang Xia: Yeah, that's it. Turn right, follow the direction of the arrow and we'll enter the subway station.

Li Hua: It's great to have easy access to the subway station from the train station.

(Li Hua and Wang Xia are at the subway entrance.)

Li Hua: There is the Suzhou Rail Transit System Map on the wall. Which line should we take to the hotel?

Wang Xia: Our hotel is near Suzhou Museum, so we can take Line 4 and get off at Beisita Station.

Li Hua: OK. Next, I guess we'll buy the subway tickets. Right?

Wang Xia: Yes. See? There's a ticket counter over there but I prefer to try the automated ticket machine nearby.

Li Hua: Frankly speaking, I don't know how to use this machine.

Wang Xia: Let me show you. First, push the button for where we want to start from.

Li Hua: That's here. (Pressing Suzhou Railway Station button)

Wang Xia: Then select the destination and press the appropriate button.

Li Hua: That's here. (Pressing Beisita Station button)

Wang Xia: Next, you can choose how many tickets you want.

Li Hua: Two.

Wang Xia: Then, it shows the fare, 4 yuan. We can pay in cash or by scanning code.

Li Hua: Let me pay by WeChat.

Wang Xia: Thanks a lot.

Li Hua: My pleasure. Oh, there're our tickets.

Wang Xia: Well. Let's take our tickets and enter the station.

Notes

1. Let's take a look at the various signs posted nearby, which will show us the way.
   让我们看看附近张贴的各种指示牌，看看怎么走。
2. Turn right, follow the direction of the arrow and we'll enter the subway station.
   向右转，沿着箭头的方向走，我们就进入地铁站了。
3. There's a ticket counter over there but I prefer to try the automated ticket machine nearby.
   那边有售票处，但我更想试试附近的自动售票机。

Part 4 Passage

Captain's Announcements（机长广播）

Boarding Announcement

Ladies and Gentlemen,

Welcome aboard Air China!

Your seat number is indicated on the edge of the overhead bin. Please put your carry-on luggage in the overhead bin or under the seat. For the convenience of others, please keep the aisle clear.

Thank you for your cooperation!

译文：登机广播

女士们、先生们：

欢迎搭乘国航航班！

当您进入客舱后，请留意行李架边缘的座位号，对号入座。客舱行李架上以及座椅下方均可以放置手提行李，请注意保持过道通畅。

谢谢您的配合！

Pre-flight Announcement

Good morning, passengers. This is your captain speaking. First, I'd like to welcome everyone on Flight CA1519. Our flight will take 2 hours and 30 minutes. To be safe, passengers are not allowed to use mobile phones or any other electronic devices throughout the flight. Laptop computers are not allowed to use during take-off and landing. We will take off immediately. Now the cabin attendants are going to have a security check. Please be seated, fasten your seat belt and make sure your seat back is straight up, your tray table is closed and your carry-on items are securely stowed in the overhead bin or under the seat. This is a non-smoking flight, please do not smoke on board. We hope you enjoy the flight!

Thank you!

译文：行前广播

各位旅客早上好，我是本次航班的机长，欢迎您乘坐 CA1519 航班。预计空中飞行时间是 2 小时 30 分钟。为了保障飞机导航及通讯系统的正常工作，在整个航程中请不要使用手机及其他电子设备。在飞机起飞和下降过程中请不要使用手提电脑，飞机很快就要起飞了，现在客舱服务人员将进行安全检查。请您坐好并系好安全带，竖直椅背和小桌板。请您确认您的手提物品是否妥善安放在头顶上方的行李架上或座椅下方。本次航班全程禁烟，在飞行途中请不要吸烟。祝您旅途愉快！

谢谢！

In-flight Announcement

Good morning, ladies and gentlemen. This is your captain speaking. We are currently cruising at an altitude of 10,000 meters at an airspeed of 620 kilometers per hour. The Fasten Seat Belt sign has been turned off and you may now leave your seat and use the washroom. However, we always recommend to keep your seat belt fastened while you're seated.

We are pleased to begin our meal services. Flight attendants will be moving through the cabin serving meals and beverages soon. For the convenience of the passenger sitting behind you, please adjust your seat back to its upright and locked position during the meal service. If you need any assistance, please contact any flight attendant.

Thank you!

译文：舱内广播

女士们、先生们，早上好。我是本次航班的机长。我们目前正以每小时

620公里的空速在10000米的高度飞行。安全带指示灯已经熄灭，现在您可以离开座位、使用洗手间。但我们仍建议您坐着的时候，系好安全带。

我们即将开始提供餐食。空乘人员将会在机舱内提供餐食及各种饮料。在用餐期间，请您调直座椅靠背至锁定位置，以方便后排的旅客。如果需要帮助，请与空乘人员联系。

谢谢！

Announcement Before Landing

Ladies and gentlemen, this is Captain speaking. We expect to land at Shanghai in 20 minutes. The estimated time of arrival will be 12:00 a.m. The local time now is 11:40 a.m. and the ground temperature is 26 degrees Celsius. Please fasten your seat belt. I would like to thank you for flying with us. I do hope you have enjoyed your flight.

Thank you!

译文：着陆前广播

女士们、先生们，这是来自机长的广播。我们预计在20分钟之后降落至上海，预计抵达时间为中午12：00，现在当地时间是11：40，气温为26℃。请您系好安全带准备降落。非常感谢您今天的搭乘，祝您愉快。

谢谢！

Announcement After Landing

Ladies and gentlemen, welcome to Shanghai Pudong International Airport. For your safety and comfort, please remain seated and keep your mobile phones powered off until the airplane has come to a complete stop. Please be sure to take all your belongings when you disembark. Your checked baggage may be claimed in the terminal building. Thank you for joining us on this trip and we are looking forward to seeing you on board again in the near future. Have a nice day!

译文：着陆后广播

各位旅客您好，欢迎抵达上海浦东国际机场。现在飞机还在滑行中，为了您的安全，请不要离开座位，同时请不要打开手机电源。下机时请拿好全部随身物品。您托运的行李物品，下机后请到候机楼出口处领取。感谢您的搭乘，我们期待着与您再一次相聚。祝您愉快！

Part 5 Exercises

Task 1 Nick is going to fly to Guangzhou. Please put the following pictures in the correct order.

________ → ________ → ________ → ________

Task 2 How to book a train ticket at China Railway's official website *www.12306.cn*? Please fill in the blanks.

Step 1 Sign up for a new account.

Step 2 ________ to your account.

Step 3 On the home page enter the departure and ________ stations, select ________ and then click the button of "Ticket Inquiry".

Step 4 Select the high-speed train number you want to book and choose ________.

Step 5 Select your seat if possible.

Step 6 Submit the order and make the ________ immediately. You can choose credit card, UnionPay (银联), WeChat Pay and Alipay.

Task 3 Lin Hai and Yang Yue are at the National Library. They're going to take the subway to the Olympic Park. How can they transfer to go there according to the following partial view of the Beijing Rail Transit Lines?

____

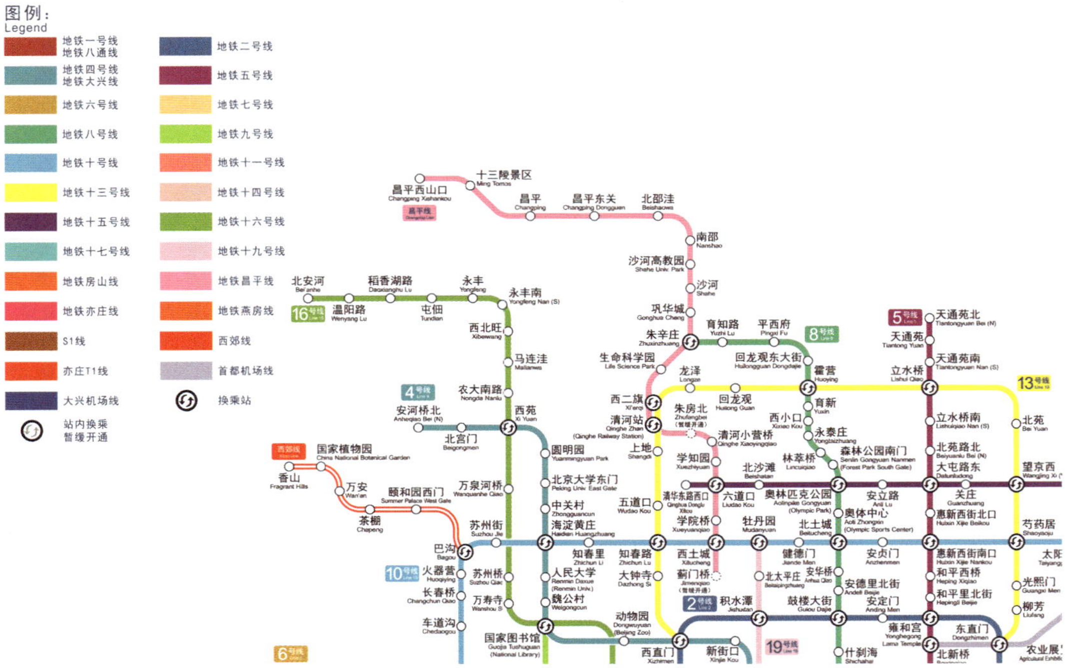

Unit 7

Task 4 Role Play

Student A: Imagine you are waiting in line at airport security.

Ask questions about what carry-on items are not allowed to go through security and board the plane.

Student B: Imagine you are an airport security officer.

Answer the passenger's questions and conduct security checks as required.

Change roles and try the role play again.

Part 6 Self- evaluation

评价项目	评价内容	自我诊断	改进措施
语言知识	I learn many common words and expressions about public transport.	□ Identifying □ Understanding □ Mastering	
认知能力	I know the steps of taking major public transport.	□ Distinction □ Merit □ Pass □ Fail	
沟通能力	I can introduce the steps of taking major public transport in English.	□ Distinction □ Merit □ Pass □ Fail	
文化意识	I get to learn about China's great achievements in public transport.	□ Increasing □ Developing □ Weakening	

Unit 7

Part 7 Culture

Building China's Impressive High-Speed Rail (Excerpt)

(from *https://www.en.qstheory.cn*, Updated: 2021-11-15)

High-speed rail (HSR) is an important indicator of the modernization of a country's transportation and a significant reflection of its level of industrialization. Despite developing HSR more than four decades later than some developed countries, thanks to the CPC'S leadership and the strengths of its system that efficiently pools national resources to achieve extraordinary feats, and the tireless efforts of several generations of railway workers, China has made historic progress in HSR, from trailing other countries, to keeping pace with the competition, and to leading the world.

China has built the world's largest and most modern HSR network.

Since the Beijing-Tianjin intercity railway—China's first train line with a design speed of 350 km/h—was completed in 2008, dozens of HSR routes have been completed and gone into service. After the 18th CPC National Congress in 2012 in particular, the development of HSR moved onto fast track, with average annual construction of 3,500 km of railway. Both the speed and quality of this construction have received global acclaim.

China has built a world-leading HSR system with independent intellectual property.

China has a complete HSR technology system consisting of three main areas: engineering construction, equipment manufacturing, and operations management. Its HSR technology is at the global forefront, and has become a world leader in a number of fields, making the significant transition from straggler to pacesetter.

Unit 8

Travelling

扫码看

Learning Objectives

After learning this unit, you should be able to:

1. get familiar with the words and expressions concerning travelling;
2. talk about travelling plans, and know how to book hotels, check in and ask directions;
3. know how to protect yourself when travelling, and understand the importance of protecting cultural relics and the environment of scenic spots.

Unit 8

Part 1 Topic Words and Expressions

扫码听

The Travel Plan

- decide on
- travel agency
- reliable
- route
- the Forbidden City
- optional
- rate
- book
- reserve
- standard room
- under the name of

At the Hotel

- reception
- key card
- kettle
- replace
- front desk
- entrance
- up to now
- unpack

On the Way to the Sights

- make an appointment
- account
- cab
- hail
- intersection
- construction
- paste

Travel Safety

- reliable
- rating
- customer feedback
- be true of
- companion
- trustworthy
- keep sb. informed of
- keep an eye on
- keep... in sight
- beware of
- adhere to
- comply with
- regulation
- scenic

Part 2 Lead-in

Li Hua, Wang Xia and their American classmate, Jack, plan to travel during the summer vacation. They need to prepare for their trip, such as making a travel plan, booking the hotel, etc. After their arrival, they check in and find something in their room is broken. On their way to the sight, they find the navigation of the online map is incorrect...

Part 3 Dialogs

Dialog 1 The Travel Plan

扫码听

(Li Hua, Wang Xia and their American classmate, Jack, are discussing their travel plan.)

Li Hua: The summer vacation is coming. Do you have any plan?

Wang Xia: I'm thinking about travelling but haven't decided on where to go.

Jack: I want to go to Beijing because I really want to visit the Great Wall.

Li Hua: Well, I travelled to Beijing several years ago and I want to go there again.

Wang Xia: Really? It's on my wish list, too! How about we go there together?

Li Hua: Great! Do we plan to go with a travel agency or on our own?

Wang Xia: A reliable travel agency is a good choice, but their schedule is always too tight. Besides, my friend is studying in Beijing, and she will stay there until the end of July. I think we could have fun together if she hang out with us at her leisure.

Jack: Perfect! Let's make a travel plan together, and book the hotel as soon as possible.

Li Hua: Let's write down our favorite attractions, and then work out our route.

(They have worked out their route.)

Wang Xia: So we're going to be there for 7 days, with the first day and the last day on the way.

Li Hua: We'll visit Tian'anmen Square, the Forbidden City, the Great Wall and Peking University. The rest are some optional sights.

Jack: We've decided to reserve the ABC Hotel because it's almost equally close to most spots. Besides, the rate of the hotel is reasonable. I'm gonna make a reservation.

(Jack dials the hotel's telephone number.)

Hotel Staff: ABC Hotel. What can I do for you?

Jack: I wanna reserve two standard rooms for seven days, starting from July 10.

Hotel Staff: May I have your name, please?

Jack: Jack Smith.

Hotel Staff: Two standard rooms from July 10 to July 16 under the name of Jack Smith. Is that right?

Jack: That's right. Thank you.

Hotel Staff: You're welcome.

Notes

1. A reliable travel agency is a good choice, but their schedule is always too tight.
   找家靠谱的旅行社是个不错的选择，但旅行社的时间安排往往很紧张。

2. Two standard rooms from July 10 to July 16 under the name of Jack Smith.
   以 Jack Smith 的名字订两间标间，入住时间是 7 月 10 日到 7 月 16 日。

Dialog 2 At the Hotel

扫码听

(On July 10, Li Hua, Wang Xia and Jack arrive at the hotel.)

Receptionist: Good afternoon. May I help you?

Jack: Good afternoon. I reserved two standard rooms under the name of Jack Smith.

Receptionist: From today to July 16, right?

Jack: Yes.

Receptionist: Could you please give me your ID cards to check in?

Jack, Wang Xia, Li Hua: Sure.

Receptionist: Please look at this camera.

(They've all checked in.)

Receptionist: You'll be in Room 301 and 302. Here are your key cards. We provide breakfast on the first floor. Have a nice stay!

Jack: Thank you.

(They enter their rooms.)

Li Hua: Oops, I'm afraid the kettle's broken. It doesn't work.

Unit 8

I'm gonna call the reception and see if they can provide a new one.

(Li Hua calls the receptionist.)

Receptionist: This is the front desk. May I help you?

Li Hua: Hi, we've just got to the room. The kettle in our room is out of order. Could you please replace it with another one?

Receptionist: I'm so sorry for that, Sir. Our staff will bring another kettle for you as soon as possible.

Li Hua: Thanks.

(Li Hua stands at the entrance of Room 302.)

Li Hua: Hey, Wang Xia. Is everything okay in your room? Our kettle has something wrong and they'll bring another one for us.

Wang Xia: Everything's fine up to now.

Li Hua: Good. Let's just get our things unpacked and have a walk around.

Wang Xia: No problem.

Notes

1. I'm gonna call the receptionist and see if they can provide a new one.

   我打电话问问前台，看他们能不能给换一个。

2. We've just got to the room. The kettle in our room is out of order.

   我们刚到房间，发现房间里的烧水壶坏了。

3. Let's just get our things unpacked and have a walk around.

   我们把行李收拾出来，然后去周围走走吧。

Dialog 3 On the Way to the Sights

扫码听

(Li Hua, Wang Xia and Jack are on their way to the sights.)

Li Hua: We need to make an appointment to visit the museum.

Wang Xia: I totally forgot that. How do we do it?

Li Hua: Just follow their WeChat official account. The reservation part is at the bottom. Then you need to fill out the form and choose the date.

Jack: It is so convenient and saves us lots of time.

Wang Xia: Well, the cab I hailed online is coming. We'll be there in 20 minutes.

(After visiting the museum, they walk to the next sight but they get lost.)

Wang Xia: I think we lose our way. The online map is incorrect.

Jack: Let me just ask... Excuse me, how do we get to the theater?

Passer-by: Well, I'm afraid it's a bit too far. You need to cross the road and go through three intersections to the south.

Jack: Thank you. It's so strange that the online map says it's right here!

Passer-by: There's road construction recently and some roads and streets are closed.

Jack: I see. Thank you so much!

Passer-by: You're welcome.

Wang Xia: Seems like a long way.

Li Hua: Why not have something to eat before going to the theater? It's time for lunch.

Wang Xia: Great. We can get some rest while eating.

Jack: How about traditional Beijing noodles with soy bean paste?

Wang Xia: Good idea.

Unit 8

Notes

1. We need to make an appointment to visit the museum.

   我们参观博物馆需要预约时间。

2. You need to cross the road and go through three intersections to the south.

   你们需要过马路，向南走三个路口。

Part 4 Passage

Travel Safety

Travel safety is closely related to our life. When we are in a totally strange city for us, how do we ensure the safety of ourselves and our property? Here are some tips.

1. Make sure that the travel agency you choose is formal and reliable. If you use travel apps, pay attention to the ratings and customers' feedback. The same is true of choosing a hotel.

2. It would be better if you travel with your parents. If not, make sure that your travelling companions are trustworthy, and keep your parents informed of your whole plan and arrangement, and keep in touch with them all the time.

3. Keep an eye on your belongings, especially your ID card, passport, bank cards, etc. When you leave the hotel, you'd better bring them with you and keep them in sight. Lock the door before sleeping.

4. Beware of forced shopping. Travel projects with super low price are likely to include forced shopping.

5. Adhere to local customs and habits, and comply with the regulations of the scenic area.

译文：旅行安全

旅行安全与我们的生活息息相关。当身处一个完全陌生的城市，如何保障我们的人身和财产安全？以下是一些小建议。

1. 确保所选的旅行社正规可靠。如果你使用的是旅行应用软件，请注意评分和顾客评价。选择酒店也如此。

2. 最好与父母一同旅行。如果没有父母陪同，请确保同行人员值得信赖，同时将旅行的计划安排告知父母，并一直与他们保持联系。

3. 注意保管好个人物品，尤其是身份证、护照、银行卡等。离开酒店时，最好随身携带以上物品并使其处于视线范围内。入睡前请锁门。

4. 警惕强制购物。价格超低的旅行项目很可能包含强制消费。

5. 遵守当地的风俗习惯和景区规定。

Part 5 Exercises

Task 1 Match the words or phrases with the pictures. Use dictionary if necessary.

1

2

Unit 8

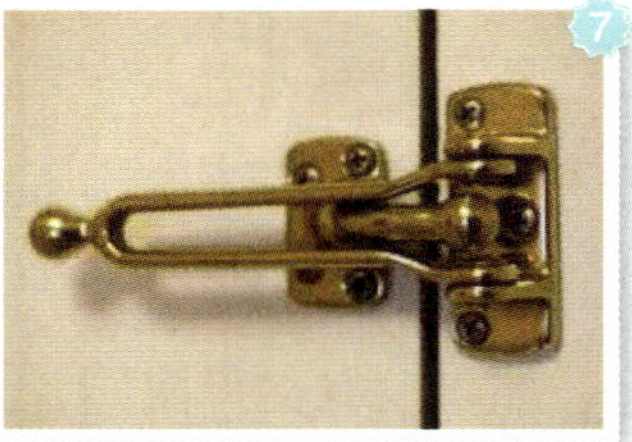

reception　kettle　sheet　hair dryer　socket　faucet　bolt　toilet paper

Task 2　Translate the following sentences into Chinese.

1. I have made a reservation and I want to check in.

____

2. We've run out of the toilet paper. Could you please bring some?

____

3. May I have an extra pillow, please?

____

4. There is no soap in the bathroom.

____

5. I wanna check out.

____

Task 3 Mat is a foreign student studying in Shandong Province. He wants to take a trip to Jinan during the holiday. Here is his plan. Please describe his plan in English.

Companion	Zhang Ning, Wang Peng, George
Time	five days: Oct. 1-Oct. 5
Transportation	high-speed train (second-class seat)
Sight	Baotu Spring, Daming Lake, Qianfo Mountain, Hongye Valley...
Hotel Room	two standard rooms with a view

Task 4 Role Play

Suppose that we are in Jiancheng Building. Please practice asking directions with your partner. For example:

Student A: Excuse me, how can I get to the canteen (Feilong Square / basketball court / dormitory / north gate / ...)?

Student B: Go straight along Xiuyuan East Road southwards. Then turn left at the Shancheng Square. It's right behind the square.

Unit 8

北
北门
重华东路
重华广场
中水处理中心
莲子湖
书昌楼
北文楼
(图书馆)
知远楼
尚勤楼
(校史馆)
工程训练中心
现代交通训练中心
闻善楼
(文化创意活动中心)
鉴诚楼
向真楼
惟实楼
(风华堂)
成美楼
行敏楼
萝谷路
敏中路
篮球场
综合训练场
田径场
滋兰西园
滋兰园
滋兰东园
任之西路
任之东路
清照西路
清照东路
飞龙广场
滋兰南园
善诚广场
餐厅
综合服务中心
校医院
学生公寓1
学生公寓2
学生公寓3
学生公寓4
学生公寓5
学生公寓6
学生公寓7

Part 6 Self- evaluation

评价项目	评价内容	自我诊断	改进措施
语言知识	I learn many common words and expressions about travelling.	☐ Identifying ☐ Understanding ☐ Mastering	
认知能力	I know how to make travel plans, book a hotel and check in.	☐ Distinction ☐ Merit ☐ Pass ☐ Fail	
沟通能力	I can talk about my travel plans, book a hotel, check in and ask directions in English.	☐ Distinction ☐ Merit ☐ Pass ☐ Fail	
文化意识	I get to learn about the importance of protecting cultural relics and the environment of scenic spots.	☐ Increasing ☐ Developing ☐ Weakening	

Unit 8

Part 7 Culture

New Guidelines for Visitors to Palace Museum (Excerpt)

(from *http://www.chinadaily.com.cn*, Updated:2023-06-16)

The Palace Museum in Beijing released new visiting guidelines to protect the World Heritage Site.

According to the guidelines, luggage cases, trolleys, scooters, bicycles and other wheeled transportation—with the exception of wheelchairs and strollers for kids—will no longer be allowed to enter the compound. Without the permission of museum authorities, commercial photography equipment, including large tripods, reflectors and camera dollies, will also be prohibited. The safety of relics and visitors is a major concern.

The Palace Museum, also known as the Forbidden City, was China's imperial palace from 1420 to 1911. Spread across 720,000 square meters in the heart of Beijing, it is seen as the zenith of ancient Chinese palatial constructions.

Following the public's enthusiasm for traditional Chinese culture in recent years, many visitors, of the younger generation in particular, like to visit the Forbidden City wearing traditional royal costumes. This trend has created a boom in the commercial photography market centering on the palace. To get better pictures, photographers often occupy visiting routes and public spaces for a long time.

The imperial garden near the Gate of Divine Prowess, the northern exit of the Palace Museum, has been affected by the heavy trolleys used to carry commercial photography equipment. The garden has become a popular area within the complex commercial photography. Its pathways are paved with pebbles set using traditional craftsmanship and are not designed to withstand the rolling of heavy trolleys. The pebbles easily loosen after being rolled over again and again. Colored glaze on the walls is also fragile and can be hit

by the trolleys.

The museum will provide an alternate plan for travelers who bring luggage because they later need to catch trains or flights. Visitors can deposit their luggage by the entry and the luggage will be transferred to the exits for pickup to save people from having to walk back, which can take more than half an hour.

Unit 9

Customs of Chinese Festivals

扫码看

Learning Objectives

After learning this unit, you should be able to:

1. get familiar with the words and expressions concerning customs of Chinese festivals;
2. introduce local customs of Chinese festivals in English;
3. know how to express the origins of customs of Chinese festivals in English.

Unit 9

Part 1 Topic Words and Expressions

扫码听

The Lantern Festival
- lantern
- inspiration
- presentation
- material
- sort out
- reunion
- entertainment
- representation
- zodiac
- symbol

The Dragon Boat Festival
- provided
- ceremony
- legend
- commemorate
- patriotic
- devour
- intangible
- heritage
- bracelet
- ornament

The Double Ninth Festival
- temple
- blast
- folk
- stall
- performance
- reluctant
- wander
- appreciate
- conception
- relevant

Poems of Chinese Festivals
- Jade
- adorn
- steed
- fragrance
- vibrate
- moth
- dedicate
- kinsfolk
- spray

Part 2 Lead-in

Wang Xia and Li Hua are discussing their presentation about customs of Chinese festivals in English.

Part 3 Dialogs

Dialog 1 The Lantern Festival

扫码听

Li Hua: Hi, what are you busy with, Wang Xia?

Wang Xia: Hey, Li Hua. I'm searching for inspirations.

Li Hua: For what?

Wang Xia: Well, my partner, you must have forgotten our presentation titled "The Story of Chinese Festivals and Me", right?

Li Hua: Er... Of course not. I guess the deadline is next Wednesday. We still have plenty of time.

Wang Xia: But we don't have enough materials. That's why I'm sorting out my album to find some suitable photos.

Li Hua: Which festival inspired you?

Wang Xia: The Lantern Festival. You know it's the day that Chinese families

get reunion to enjoy sweet dumplings and various folk entertainments.

Li Hua: Yeah, I like the round dumplings, not only for its delicious taste but also for its representation of reunion and happiness.

Wang Xia: And my whole family goes to Baotu Spring almost every year to enjoy lanterns after a big meal.

Li Hua: So, did you go there this year?

Wang Xia: Certainly. We also took a few photos. Look! How about this one?

Li Hua: Wow, I like it! The giant dragon lantern in this photo is nearly a work of art!

Wang Xia: Really? I'm keen on dragon, too. It is not only one of the Chinese twelve zodiac signs, but also a symbol of the Chinese spirit.

Li Hua: Any others? Let me enjoy more.

Wang Xia: However, I couldn't take more pictures.

Li Hua: Oh, what a pity!

Wang Xia: Yes, indeed. Can we use them directly?

Li Hua: Listen. I hit on an idea.

Wang Xia: Go ahead.

Li Hua: Why not we go out to take some photos this weekend? The Dragon Boat Festival is coming. I know there will be a Dragon Boat Race at Daming Lake.

Wang Xia: Really? That's a great idea!

Notes

1. What are you busy with?

   你在忙什么呢?

2. It's the day that Chinese families get reunion to enjoy sweet dumplings and various folk entertainments.

   这一天，家家户户团聚在一起吃汤圆、参加各种民间娱乐项目。

3. It is not only one of the Chinese twelve zodiac signs, but also a symbol of the Chinese spirit.

   它不仅是十二生肖之一，也是中华民族精神的象征。

Dialog 2 The Dragon Boat Festival

扫码听

Li Hua: Provided that you have agreed with me, let's make some preparations.

Wang Xia: Well. Tell me your plan.

Li Hua: First, let's confirm when and where the race will be held.

Wang Xia: Sure, but how?

Li Hua: Check it online, of course.

Wang Xia: Okay, let me search for it. En... The official website says the opening ceremony will be held at 8:00 a.m. on Saturday morning at Daming Lake.

Li Hua: 8:00 a.m.? It's quite early!

Wang Xia: Obviously. The race will begin at 8:30 a.m.

Li Hua: If we set out earlier, we should be able to watch it.

Wang Xia: Sure. Now let's schedule a meeting at the school gate at 7:00 a.m. on Saturday morning.

Li Hua: No problem.

Wang Xia: Is there anything else?

Unit 9

Li Hua: Then, how much do you know about the Dragon Boat Festival?

Wang Xia: Well, as we all know, it is also called the Duanwu Fesitival, which falls on the fifth day of the fifth lunar month. Legend has it that it was the day when Qu Yuan threw himself into the Miluo River and died for his beloved homeland.

Li Hua: In order to commemorate this patriotic poet, the customs of holding dragon boat races and throwing *Zongzi* into the river on the fifth day of the fifth lunar month were passed down.

Wang Xia: Why did they throw *Zongzi* into the river?

Li Hua: Well, it is said that the ancients threw rice dumplings and other food into the Miluo River to keep fish and turtles from devouring Qu Yuan's body.

Wang Xia: Oh, is that so?

Li Hua: You bet. You know, as China's first festival to be selected as the World Intangible Cultural Heritage, it has so many customs.

Wang Xia: For example?

Li Hua: You can wear bracelets or *Zongzi* shaped ornaments made of five-color threads to pray for good luck and drive away evils.

Wang Xia: I remember my mother used to make it for me when I was a child.

Li Hua: Me too.

Wang Xia: I guess we can make some to wear while watching the race!

Li Hua: Why not?

Notes

1. Provided that you have agreed with me, let's make some preparations.
既然我们意见一致，那就来做些准备吧。

2. Legend has it that it was the day when Qu Yuan threw himself into the Miluo River and died for his beloved homeland.
相传这是屈原投身汨罗江，以身殉国的日子。

3. You can wear bracelets or *Zongzi* shaped ornaments made of five-color threads to pray for good luck and drive away evils.
你可以佩戴五色丝线制成的手环或粽子形状的饰品来祈福驱邪。

Dialog 3 The Double Ninth Festival

扫码听

Li Hua: Now we have two choices for our presentation: the Lantern Festival or the Dragon Boat Festival.

Wang Xia: Yeah, I also have another plan.

Li Hua: Great. Success and opportunity are always for those who are well-prepared!

Wang Xia: So, what about the Double Ninth Festival?

Li Hua: You mean Chongyang Festival?

Wang Xia: Yes, the festival is famous for the poem titled "On Double Ninth Day Thinking of My Brothers at Home".

Li Hua: It's really a nice choice!

Wang Xia: I heard that the temple fair on Qianfo Mountain is very fun every Double Ninth Festival.

Unit 9

Li Hua: Aha, it's true. I accompanied my grandfather there last year. It was a blast! The interesting folk stalls and performances made me reluctant to leave!

Wang Xia: Really? I haven't been there yet. I don't enjoy climbing mountains.

Li Hua: Then I strongly recommend you give it a try this Double Ninth Festival. Wandering through the stalls while climbing, you will not feel tired at all!

Wang Xia: Em... Maybe I should have a try. After all, climbing mountains is one of most important customs on the Double Ninth Day.

Li Hua: Definitely.

Wang Xia: However, the festival is still several months away. Do you have any relevant materials available?

Li Hua: Yes, I took many photos and videos with my grandpa. I can pack them and transfer the package to you.

Wang Xia: That's great!

Notes

1. *On Double Ninth Day Thinking of My Brothers at Home*

《九月九日忆山东兄弟》

2. The interesting folk stalls and performances made me reluctant to leave!

有趣的民俗小摊和表演让我流连忘返！

Part 4 Passage

The Lantern Festival Night—to the Tune of Green Jade Table

by Xin Qiji

One night's east wind adorns a thousand trees with flowers,
And blows down stars in showers.
Fine steeds and carved cabs spread fragrance en route;
Music vibrates from the flute;
The moon sheds its full light,
While fish and dragon lanterns dance all night.
In gold-thread dress, with moth or willow ornaments,
Giggling, she melts into the throng with trails of scents.
But in the crowd once and again,
I look for her in vain.
When all at once I turn my head,
I find her there where lantern light is dimly shed.

—Translated by Xu Yuanchong

原词：

青玉案・元夕

辛弃疾

东风夜放花千树，更吹落，星如雨。宝马雕车香满路。凤箫声动，玉壶光转，一夜鱼龙舞。

蛾儿雪柳黄金缕，笑语盈盈暗香去。众里寻他千百度，蓦然回首，那人却在，灯火阑珊处。

Unit 9

Dragon Boat Day

by Wen Xiu

Whom was the Dragon Boat Day first dedicated to?
For many centuries it's been held to be Qu Yuan.
I would laugh at this vast, but aimless River Chu
For not washing off the wrongs done to the righteous one.

—Translated by Qin Dachuan

原诗：

端　午

文　秀

节分端午自谁言，万古传闻为屈原。
堪笑楚江空渺渺，不能洗得直臣冤。

On Double Ninth Day Thinking of My Brothers at Home

by Wang Wei

Alone, a lonely stranger in a foreign land;
I doubly pine for my kinsfolk on a holiday.
I know my brothers would, with dogwood sprays in hand;
Climb up mountains and miss me so far away.

—Translated by Xu YuanChong

原诗：

九月九日忆山东兄弟

王　维

独在异乡为异客，每逢佳节倍思亲。
遥知兄弟登高处，遍插茱萸少一人。

Part 5 Exercises

Task 1 Please try to name the related Chinese festivals according to the following customs shown in the pictures.

1.________________

2.________________

3.________________

Unit 9

Task 2 This passage is about TCM (traditional Chinese medicine) suggestions of the Pure Brightness. Please complete it with the words below.

absorb	stomach	honor	suggested	suitable

The Pure Brightness is the 5th solar term. It's the day to visit the tombs of ancestors, dead relatives and friends to 1.________ them. The traditional Chinese medical theory believes that this period is the perfect time for people to 2.________ Yang Qi into human's body. People are 3.________ to take more exercises such as jogging, gymnastics, hiking. Although the old custom of eating cold food is still popular in some areas, not everyone's body is 4.________ for doing so, especially those who have weak 5.________. People should eat more fruits and vegetables such as chives, Chinese cabbage, and radish.

Task 3 Please decide whether the following statements about Chinese festivals are TRUE or FALSE. If it is false, please tell us the reason.

(True/False) 1. Ancient people also called the Lantern Festival, which falls on the 15th of the first month of the lunar calendar, Shangyuan Festival.

(True/False) 2. Qingming Festival is usually around the fifth day of the fourth lunar month.

(True/False) 3. People are accustomed to appreciating chrysanthemums on the Dragon Boat Festival.

(True/False) 4. Qixi, the seventh evening of the seventh month of the lunar calendar, is the time when the Cowherd and the Weaving Maid meet in Heaven every year according to a legend.

(True/False) 5. Mid-Autumn Festival is on the 15th day of the eighth month of the lunar calendar, which is customary to enjoy the moon and eat moon cakes.

Task 4 Role Play

Student A: Imagine you are a foreigner travelling to China.

Ask questions about some famous Chinese attractions and local customs.

Student B: Imagine you are a local guide.

Answer your tourist's questions and introduce the unique customs here.

Change roles and try the role play again.

Unit 9

Part 6 Self- evaluation

评价项目	评价内容	自我诊断	改进措施
语言知识	I learn many useful words and expressions about customs of Chinese festivals.	☐ Identifying ☐ Understanding ☐ Mastering	
认知能力	I can obtain and understand the information about the customs of Chinese festivals in English.	☐ Distinction ☐ Merit ☐ Pass ☐ Fail	
沟通能力	I can introduce customs of Chinese festivals in English.	☐ Distinction ☐ Merit ☐ Pass ☐ Fail	
文化意识	I get to have a further understanding of the glorious long history of Chinese traditional culture.	☐ Increasing ☐ Developing ☐ Weakening	

Part 7 Culture

The Chinese Zodiac/Animal of the Year (Excerpt)

(from *https://www.chinesesethought.cn/EN*, Updated: 2019-07-04)

Shengxiao in Chinese refers to the twelve animals that make up the Chinese Zodiac.

The ancient Chinese included in this list eleven animals closely associated with farming, plus the dragon, a legendary animal which has cultural symbolic meaning in China. They were then associated with the twelve Earthly Branches (in a twelve-year cycle) to each represent a year. Thus a person's year of birth is also associated with a specific animal.

Combining the Zodiac with the Branches produces the following order: *zishu* (rat), *chouniu* (ox), *yinhu* (tiger), *maotu* (rabbit), *chenlong* (dragon), *sishe* (snake), *wuma* (horse), *weiyang* (sheep), *shenhou* (monkey), *youji* (rooster), *xugou* (dog), and *haizhu* (pig).

The Zodiac had already entered into use by the Eastern Han Dynasty, and has been a distinctive feature of Chinese culture and folk tradition ever since. Today, the influence of the Chinese Zodiac culture can still be found in the tradition of a person's animal birth year and marriage, during festivals and in folk arts, like paper-cutting.

Unit 10

China's Achievements

扫码看

Learning Objectives

After learning this unit, you should be able to:

1. get familiar with the words and expressions concerning mobile payment, modern agriculture and space technology;
2. introduce briefly China's major achievements in mobile payment, modern agriculture and space technology in English;
3. know that after decades of hard work, Chinese people have achieved world-renowned achievements in many fields.

Unit 10

Part 1 Topic Words and Expressions

扫码听

Mobile Payment

- coincidence
- achievement
- field
- mobile payment
- tap
- customer
- experience
- payment tool
- impact
- cashless society
- payment habit

Space Technology

- space technology
- launch
- manned spacecraft
- civilian astronaut
- dynamics and control technology
- aerospace system
- spaceflight
- crew
- space station
- spacewalk

Modern Agriculture

- modern agriculture
- stable
- grain
- agricultural product
- arable land
- food security
- modernization
- advance
- diversification
- digitalization

Yuan Longping

- agronomist
- hybrid rice
- variety
- rice output
- diluted
- high-yielding
- strain
- rice paddy
- self-sufficiency
- salt-alkali

Part 2 Lead-in

Next month, an English speech contest on the topic of "China's Achievements" will be held in the college. Students discuss the contest after class.

Part 3 Dialogs

扫码听

Dialog 1 Mobile Payment

(At the school café, Wang Xia meets Xiao Qi, a member from the English club.)

Wang Xia: Xiao Qi! Hi, fancy meeting you here.

Xiao Qi: Wang Xia! What a coincidence!

Wang Xia: I often come here after classes.

Xiao Qi: Sounds good. Have you ordered?

Wang Xia: I was just about to.

(After ordering coffee, they sit together and talk.)

Wang Xia: How have you been?

Xiao Qi: Pretty good. I'm preparing for the English speech contest next month.

Wang Xia: I've never heard of it. What is it?

Xiao Qi: You know, I'm a member of the English club. Next month, an English speech contest on the topic of "China's Achievements" will be held, and all club members are required to attend.

Wang Xia: Sounds interesting! Which industry or field are you going to talk about?

Xiao Qi: I intend to talk about the achievements in mobile payment, which is very convenient for us.

Wang Xia: Indeed. The wallet is no longer in use. We can buy whatever we want simply with a tap of the smart phone.

Xiao Qi: Mobile payment has become very common in our lives and has improved customer experience.

Wang Xia: This is really a good topic. What will your speech consist of?

Xiao Qi: I'm going to start my speech with the introduction of how to use mobile payment tools.

Wang Xia: Good idea! Though we use mobile payment every day, most people may not be able to describe the steps in English.

Xiao Qi: Next, I would like to introduce the impact of mobile payment—the cashless society.

Wang Xia: It has been a hot topic. Do you think cash will disappear in the near future?

Xiao Qi: That is what I want to talk about in the last part of my speech. When it comes to China's senior citizens, most of them prefer to use cash in their daily lives. We should respect consumers' payment habits.

Wang Xia: You have made enough preparation for the speech contest. You can definitely win the prize!

Notes

1. We can buy whatever we want simply with a tap of the smart phone.
   只需点击一下智能手机，我们就可以买到想要的任何东西。
2. Mobile payment has become very common in our lives and has improved customer experience.
   移动支付在我们的生活中变得非常普遍，并且改善了用户体验。
3. When it comes to China's senior citizens, most of them prefer to use cash in their daily lives.
   对中国的老年人而言，他们大多更喜欢在日常生活中使用现金。

Dialog 2 Modern Agriculture

扫码听

(Li Hua and Peter, an overseas student, are talking about the English speech contest at the entrance to the library.)

Peter: You're Li Hua, aren't you?

Li Hua: Yes. Glad to see you.

Peter: I'm Peter, the overseas student. We met at the club.

Li Hua: Hi, Peter. What are you doing here? Do you want to borrow some books?

Peter: I'm preparing for the English speech, but I still need more specific information. Oh, can I talk to you for a second?

Li Hua: Sure. My pleasure.

Peter: I plan to introduce China's achievements in modern agriculture. Since I come from a developing country, I know that agriculture is important.

Li Hua: It is true. Ensuring stable and safe supplies of grain and other important agricultural products is always the top priority for China.

Peter: Also, it is mentioned in some articles that China has succeeded in producing about one-fourth of the world's grain and feeding about one-fifth of the world's population with less than 10% of the world's arable land.

Li Hua: As a Chinese, I'm really proud of it.

Peter: I think this is a great achievement in the pursuit of food security not only in China itself but also globally.

Li Hua: The government has been increasing investment to speed up the modernization of agricultural production. Recent developments in the agricultural industry, therefore, could be a major part of your speech in addition to the general introduction.

Peter: Excellent idea! Could you give me some more specific suggestions?

Li Hua: In my opinion, the key to advancing agricultural modernization lies in the development of technology. Diversification and digitalization are two words mentioned frequently in the news.

Peter: Thank you so much for your advice. It's very kind of you.

Li Hua: It's a pleasure. Well, let's go into the library and find more information from books.

Notes

1. Ensuring stable and safe supplies of grain and other important agricultural products is always the top priority for China.
确保粮食和其他重要农产品的稳定安全供应始终是中国的首要任务。

2. Also, it is mentioned in some articles that China has succeeded in producing about one-fourth of the world's grain and feeding one-fifth of the world's population with less than 10% of the world's arable land.

此外，一些文章也提到，中国以占不到世界 10% 的耕地，生产出世界约四分之一的粮食，养活了世界五分之一的人口。

3. The government has been increasing investment to speed up the modernization of agricultural production.

   政府一直在增加投资，以加快农业生产的现代化。

4. In my opinion, the key to advancing agricultural modernization lies in the development of technology.

   在我看来，推进农业现代化的关键在于技术的发展。

Dialog 3 Space Technology

扫码听

(Before the club activities, several members of the English club watch short videos together.)

Wang Xia: Hey, guess what short video I got.

Mat: What is it?

Wang Xia: Headline news today! The *Shenzhou XVI* Spacecraft was launched successfully.

Mat: Let me watch it too.

(After watching the short video, Wang Xia and Mat talk about it.)

Mat: *Shenzhou XVI* is a manned spacecraft. How cool it is!

Wang Xia: Yeah, and it sent China's first civilian astronaut to space.

Mat: What is his name?

Wang Xia: Gui Haichao. He grew up in a family in southwest China's Yunnan province, whose long-held dream was to fly to space. Now his dream has become a reality.

Mat: He seems to be a professor.

Wang Xia: Yes. He is a professor who specializes in spacecraft dynamics and control technology for aerospace systems.

Mat: The other two astronauts are Jing Haipeng and Zhu Yangzhu.

Wang Xia: Do you remember? The short video says it is Jing's fourth spaceflight, making him China's most experienced astronaut.

Mat: He's the hero astronaut.

Wang Xia: The *Shenzhou XVI* crew members will move into China's Tiangong space station to meet their peers from the *Shenzhou XV* mission. They will stay inside the Tiangong space station for around five months and carry out several spacewalks and do some experiments.

Mat: Amazing! China's space technology has made such remarkable achievements. Perhaps I can introduce it in the coming English speech contest.

Notes

1. He is a professor who specializes in spacecraft dynamics and control technology for aerospace systems.
   他是一名专门研究航天器动力学与航天系统控制技术的教授。

2. The *Shenzhou XVI* crew members will move into China's Tiangong space station to meet their peers from the *Shenzhou XV* mission.
   神舟十六号的航天员将进入中国天宫空间站，与神舟十五号的航天员会面。
3. They will stay inside the Tiangong space station for around five months and carry out several spacewalks and do some experiments.
   他们将在天宫空间站停留大约五个月，进行几次太空行走并做一些实验。

Part 4 Passage

Yuan Longping

Yuan Longping (1930–2021) is a Chinese agronomist known for pioneering the development of the world's first hybrid rice varieties which significantly improved China's rice output and food security.

His dedication to rice production increase to feed the people dates back to the mid-20th century when China was going through a tough time. "My life goal is to help all people stay away from hunger." In 1973, he cultivated the world's first high-yielding hybrid rice strain, which could reach a yield of over 500 kg from previous 300 kg per *mu* (0.067 hectares). Such rice varieties not only give higher yield but also reduce the plant area needed without sacrificing the quality of the rice.

As a result, China's total rice output increased from 5.69 billion tons in 1950 to 19.47 billion tons in 2000. Nowadays, the hybrid rice is grown in almost half of China's rice paddies and its yield makes up for 60 percent of the country's total rice production. According to China's second white paper on food security in 2019, China has basically achieved self-sufficiency in grain supply. In terms of rice, there's a surplus in production, the paper said.

So far, the hybrid varieties he developed have been grown extensively in over 40 countries, including the U.S., Brazil, India, Vietnam, the Philippines,

Madagascar and others. In the meantime, he was also engaged in cultivating salt-alkali tolerant rice, bringing rice grown in diluted seawater to people's table.

In 2019, Yuan, academician with both the Chinese Academy of Engineering and the U.S. National Academy of Sciences, was awarded with Medal of the Republic, China's highest honor, for his groundbreaking research.

译文：袁隆平

中国农学家袁隆平（1930—2021）率先培育出世界上第一个杂交水稻品种，这大大提高了中国的水稻产量和粮食安全。

他致力于增加水稻产量以养活人民，这可以追溯到20世纪中期，当时中国正处于艰难时期。“我的人生目标是帮助所有人远离饥饿。”1973年，他培育了世界上第一个高产杂交水稻品种，亩产量从以前的300千克提高到500千克以上。这样的水稻品种不仅产量高，而且在不牺牲水稻品质的情况下减少了所需的种植面积。

因此，中国的稻米总产量从1950年的56.9亿吨增加到2000年的194.7亿吨。如今，中国几乎一半的稻田都种植杂交水稻，其产量占全国水稻总产量的60%。根据2019年中国第二份粮食安全白皮书，中国已基本实现粮食自给自足。白皮书称，就大米而言，产量存在过剩的情况。

到目前为止，他开发的杂交品种已在40多个国家广泛种植，包括美国、巴西、印度、越南、菲律宾、马达加斯加等。同时，他还从事耐盐碱水稻的种植，将在稀释海水中种植的大米带到人们的餐桌上。

2019年，中国工程院院士、美国国家科学院院士袁隆平因其开创性的研究而被授予中国最高荣誉——共和国勋章。

Part 5 Exercises

Task 1 Jimmy is a new overseas student, who would like to download and use mobile payment tool. Please help him put the following steps in the correct order.

1

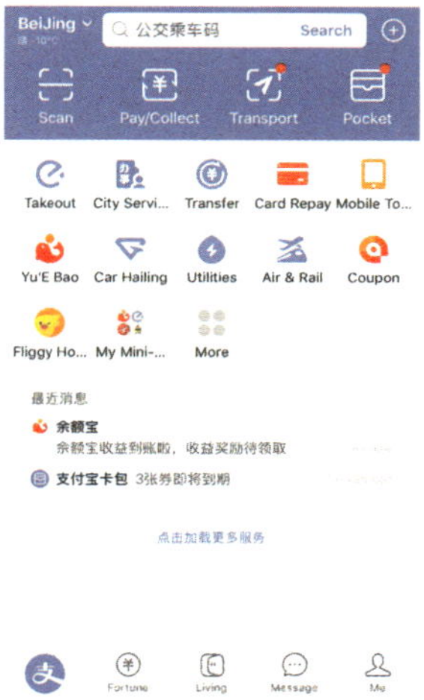

2

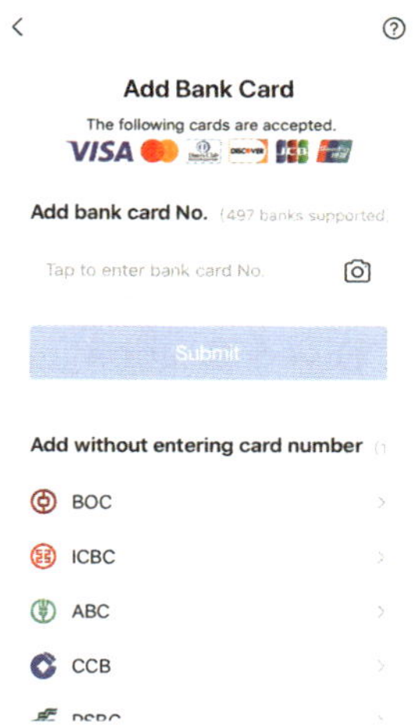

3

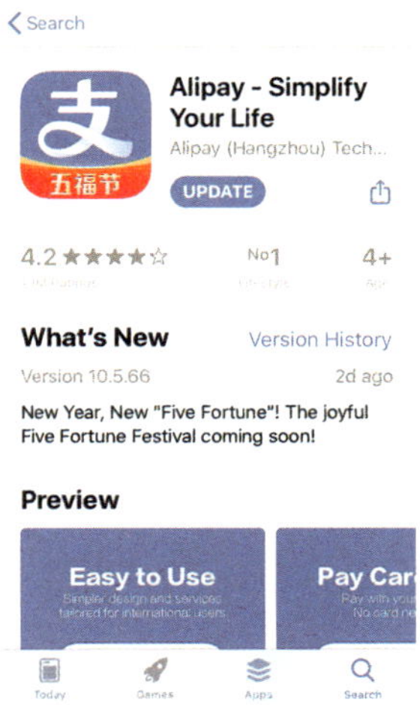

4

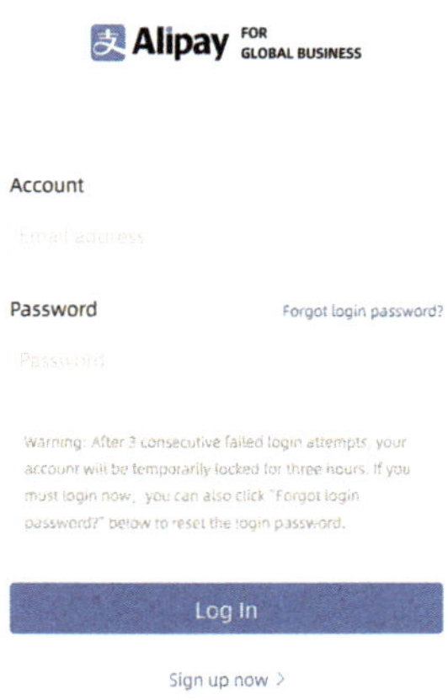

________ → ________ → ________ → ________

Task 2 Read the following statements and decide whether they are TRUE or FALSE according to Dialogue 2.

(True/False) 1. China has succeeded in producing about one-fourth of the world's grain.

(True/False) 2. China's arable land accounts for more than 10% of that of the world's arable land.

(True/False) 3. Chinese government has been increasing investment to speed up the modernization of agricultural production.

(True/False) 4. The key to advancing agricultural modernization lies in learning from foreign countries.

(True/False) 5. Diversification and digitalization are two words mentioned frequently in the news.

Task 3 Please fill in the blanks according to Dialogue 3.

1. The headline news today reports that the *Shenzhou XVI* Spacecraft __________ (发射) successfully.
2. The *Shenzhou XVI* is a __________ (载人航天器).
3. It is Jing Haipeng's fourth __________ (太空飞行), making him China's most experienced astronaut.
4. The *Shenzhou XVI* crew members will move into China's Tiangong __________ (空间站) to meet their peers from the *Shenzhou XV* mission.
5. The crew members will stay inside the Tiangong space station for about five months and carry out several __________ (太空行走) and do some experiments.

Task 4 Role Play

Student A: Imagine you are a member of the English club and will participate in the English speech contest on the topic of "China's Achievements".

Please give a speech in public.

Student B: Imagine you are a student. Listen to Student A's speech and give a brief summary.

Change roles and try the role play again.

Unit 10

Part 6 Self-evaluation

评价项目	评价内容	自我诊断	改进措施
语言知识	I learn many common words and expressions about mobile payment, modern agriculture and space technology.	☐ Identifying ☐ Understanding ☐ Mastering	
认知能力	I know the trend of mobile payment, the development of modern agriculture, and the latest achievements of manned space technology in China.	☐ Distinction ☐ Merit ☐ Pass ☐ Fail	
沟通能力	I can introduce briefly China's major achievements in mobile payment, modern agriculture and space technology in English.	☐ Distinction ☐ Merit ☐ Pass ☐ Fail	
文化意识	I get to learn about that China has achieved world-renowned achievements in many fields.	☐ Increasing ☐ Developing ☐ Weakening	

Part 7 Culture

China Leads Acceleration in Global Digital Race (Excerpt)

(from *https://www.chinadaily.com.cn,* Updated: 2023-07-14)

BEIJING—China has seen a significant increase in the size of its digital economy over the past seven years, amid an accelerated development of the global digital economy.

According to a research report released on July 5 at the main forum of the Global Digital Economy Conference 2023 in Beijing, the scale of China's digital economy increased by \$4.1 trillion from 2016 to 2022, with a compound annual growth rate of 14.2 percent.

The scale of China's digital economy grew to 50.2 trillion yuan (\$6.96 trillion) in 2022.

The share of the digital economy in the country's GDP rose to 41.5 percent, making it an important engine for stable growth and transformation.

Currently, countries around the world are speeding up the development of key areas of the digital economy, and actively seizing development opportunities in fields such as digital technologies and industries, industrial digitalization and data elements.

Unit 11

Job Hunting

扫码看

Learning Objectives

After learning this unit, you should be able to:

1. get familiar with the words and expressions about job hunting;
2. answer common questions in a job interview, and talk about the reason for your choice of work;
3. know how to make a resume and protect yourself when looking for a job, and know that creative job fairs are emerging in China.

Unit 11

Part 1 Topic Words and Expressions

扫码听

The Resume

- resume
- perfection
- degree
- internship
- relevant
- reverse
- chronological
- certificate
- prepare for
- interviewer

The Interview

- usher
- orderly
- collaborate with
- modelling
- social insurance
- housing fund
- meal allowance
- annual vacation
- probation period
- paid vacation
- maximum
- salary expectation
- pre-tax salary

Choice of Work

- offer
- pros and cons
- offset
- from scratch
- position
- up to sb.

Job-hunting Safety

- competitive
- ignore
- numerous
- disguise as
- deposit
- trick
- transfer... to...
- endanger
- recommend
- discern
- impressive

Part 2 Lead-in

This is the last year of their college life. Li Hua and Wang Xia are looking for a job. They talk about how to make a resume, prepare for the interview, and choose their jobs.

Part 3 Dialogs

Dialog 1 The Resume

扫码听

Li Hua: How's your resume going?

Wang Xia: I'm almost done. I'm working on its perfection.

Li Hua: You're so efficient. I haven't started yet. How do you make your resume?

Wang Xia: Well, first, you need to give your personal information, such as name, telephone number, e-mail... It's important to make sure that they are noticed.

Li Hua: Okay. And education background is also important, I guess?

Wang Xia: Yes. I write it starting from high school, and then our college, including time period and final degree.

Unit 11

Li Hua: Did you list your internship experience? I think it helps a lot if you have relevant job experience.

Wang Xia: Sure. I've written them down in a reverse chronological order.

Li Hua: It'd be much better if you explain what you've done and what results you've achieved, using specific data.

Wang Xia: You're right! That helps a lot! And I need to list my certificates and awards.

Li Hua: Do you have any target company?

Wang Xia: Yes, I've searched on a job-hunting website, choosing three target companies. Two of them are local and the third is in Beijing. And I want to apply for other possible companies as well.

Li Hua: Great. I guess you need to prepare for the interview in the next few days.

Wang Xia: Yeah. I'll go to their official websites to learn more about the companies, and think of questions that the interviewers may ask. By the way, the on-campus recruitment will be held this weekend.

Li Hua: Well, I must make my resume as soon as I can.

Wang Xia: It's a lot of pressure, you know, to find a job.

Li Hua: Don't worry.

Notes

1. It's important to make sure that they are noticed.

   重要的是要把这些信息置于醒目的位置。

2. I've written them down in a reverse chronological order.

   我将实习经历按照时间顺序由近及远列出来了。

3. Do you have any target company?

   你有什么目标公司吗？

Dialog 2 The Interview

(Wang Xia arrives at the company. The HR assistant ushers her into Meeting Room 3.)

扫码听

HR Assistant: Good afternoon, Wang Xia. Nice to meet you!

Wang Xia: Good afternoon. Nice to meet you!

HR Assistant: Well, the interviewers are at a meeting. I'm afraid it's gonna be another 5 minutes to finish. Just wait a minute and I'll get you some water.

Wang Xia: Okay, thank you.

(Five minutes later, the interviewers are coming. They are Steve, the department manager of ABC company, and Chloe, the HR director of the company.)

Steve: Hi, Wang Xia. I'm Steve. I'm the department manager and this is Chloe, our HR director.

Wang Xia: Hi. It's really nice to meet you.

Chloe: Hello.

Steve: So we've seen your resume. It's really nice that you has relevant job experience. Let me just ask something about yourself. What do you think is your biggest strength in your personality?

Wang Xia: I think my biggest strength in my personality is patience, and this quality is important to the position I apply for. In my last internship, I need to deal with different kinds of people, and I always finish the task in a very orderly way.

Steve: Have you ever worked in a team? We have much teamwork, so we hope that you could collaborate with other colleagues.

Wang Xia: Yes. I was an active member of the Mathematical Modelling

Society in our college. We used to work as a team to solve math problems and I was a team leader, so I cooperated with as well as led my team members. Our team won several awards as mentioned in my resume. So yes, I like and I'm good at working with people.

Steve: Wonderful. Do you have any questions about our company?

Wang Xia: Well, I want to know more about the benefits for staff.

Chloe: Sure. We provide our staff with social insurance and housing fund, and an extra commercial insurance, which is not included in many companies. Plus, a meal allowance of ¥100 is offered as well. And you'll receive birthday gift every year.

Wang Xia: What about annual vacation?

Chloe: After the probation period, you'll have seven days of paid vacation every year. It'll add one more day per year, with the maximum of fifteen days. And, of course, if you don't use them up in one year, they'll roll over to the next year.

Wang Xia: That sounds great.

Steve: So, what's your salary expectation?

Wang Xia: Well, I hope my pre-tax salary could be ¥5000 per month.

Steve: Sounds reasonable.

Notes

1. In my last internship, I need to deal with different kinds of people, and I always finish the task in a very orderly way.

在我的上一份实习工作中，我需要与各种各样的人打交道，我总能井井有条地完成任务。

2. We provide our staff with social insurance and housing fund, and an extra commercial insurance, which is not included in many companies.
我们为员工提供社保和住房公积金，此外还会额外提供一份商业保险，这在很多公司是没有的。
3. And, of course, if you don't use them up in one year, they'll roll over to the next year.
当然，如果你在一年内没有用完年假，剩余部分会顺延到下一年。

Dialog 3 Choice of Work

扫码听

(Li Hua and Wang Xia have passed interviews of the companies they applied for. They are discussing which offer to accept.)

Li Hua: I heard you pass the interviews of two companies. Congrats!
Wang Xia: Same to you! Have you decided which one to accept?
Li Hua: Not yet. Honestly, I can't make up my mind because they all have their pros and cons.
Wang Xia: Like?
Li Hua: For example, the first one gives a higher salary, but it's in another city, where the living cost is also high.
Wang Xia: Well, I guess that offsets the high salary.
Li Hua: Right. And to live in another city means you have to rebuild your social circle from scratch.
Wang Xia: That's a little bit of challenge. You need to think about renting a house, going to the hospital alone... But that won't be a problem for you, I think. What about the other company?
Li Hua: The other is a local one. It's not far from my home with a fair salary. But the biggest problem is, they offer me another position instead of the one I applied for. And this job is less relevant to my major.

Wang Xia: That's really hard to decide. You have to think about what you really want.

Li Hua: Yeah... What about you? Have you made your decision?

Wang Xia: Well, my case is much simpler. I took three interviews: two passed, and one I didn't get any information—I guess that means "no". The two companies are of similar scale, offering the same position with the same salary, so I choose the one that's nearer.

Li Hua: Sounds great. For me, it's hard to make a choice.

Wang Xia: It's also a chance to know yourself. You could ask some advice from your parents and teachers. But in the end, it's up to you.

Li Hua: Thanks for your suggestion.

Notes

1. And to live in another city means you have to rebuild your social circle from scratch.
   在另一个城市工作意味着你要从零开始建立自己的社交圈。
2. But the biggest problem is, they offer me another position instead of the one I applied for.
   但最大的问题是，他们提供的是另一个职位，不是我之前申请的那个。
3. The two companies are of similar scale, offering the same position with the same salary.
   两家公司规模相当，提供了相同的职位，薪资也一样。

Part 4 Passage

Job-hunting Safety

Looking for a job is not so easy. Job market is increasingly competitive these years. When you are busy in making your resume and preparing the interview, there is one thing that is of great importance but likely to be ignored—safety.

Job platforms provide numerous job chances for us every day. However, not all of them are "real". Some are just disguised as "job chances". For instance, if they say you need to pay deposit, it's likely to be a con. Other tricks are like, "Our company is abroad; you need to pay for the plane to take the interview" , or "We have bought you a train ticket and you need to pay for it". This is much worse because there's probably no such a company and they just want to transfer you to another country, endangering your life.

So, how to find a job safely?

Well, the most recommended platform is campus recruitment. Your college could make sure that the companies are formal. Besides, you can pay attention to the recruitment section on the official website of large companies. If you want to use job websites, please be very careful to discern various job information, especially a position with low threshold but impressive salary.

译文：求职安全

找工作并非易事，如今的招聘市场竞争愈发激烈。在你忙着做简历、准备面试的时候，有一件十分重要却往往被忽略的事情——安全。

招聘平台每天为我们提供了不计其数的岗位，但并非所有岗位都是“真实的”，有的只是伪装成了“工作机会”。比如，如果他们说你需要支付押金，那大概率是个骗局。还有其他骗术，比如，“我们公司在国外，你需要购买机票来参加面试”，“我们已经为你购买了火车票，需要你支付一下”。这种情况更糟，因为也许根本没有这样一家公司，对方只是想把你转移到异国他乡，威胁你的人身安全。

那么，如何在找工作的时候确保安全呢?

其实，最值得推荐的平台还是校园招聘。学校可以确保参加校园招聘的企业都是正规企业。此外，可以留意一下大公司网站的招聘板块。如果你想使用招聘网站的话，请一定仔细甄别工作信息，尤其是那种低门槛、高收入的岗位。

Part 5 Exercises

Task 1 This is an Employment Application Form the HR gives you before you start your interview. Please complete it with your information.

Employment Application Form

Position of Interest				(Photo)
Position		Expected Salary		

Personal Information				
Name		Gender	☐ Male ☐ Female	
Nationality		Place of Birth		
Date of Birth (MM/DD/YY)	______/____/____	Age		
ID Type	☐ Passport ☐ ID Card ☐ Exit & Entry Permit		ID Number	
Email			Mobile Number	______________
Residential Address				

Educational Background					
Education & Training	Name of School	From MM/YY To MM/YY	Major Studies	Certificate	Status
University/ College					☐ Completed ☐ Not Completed ☐ In Progress
High School					☐ Completed ☐ Not Completed ☐ In Progress
Others					☐ Completed ☐ Not Completed ☐ In Progress

Working History					
Are you currently employed?	☐ Yes ☐ No				
Working Period	From	(M)	(Y) To	(M)	(Y)
Company		Telephone Number			
Title					
Job Responsibilities					

Professional Skills

Language Skills			
Language	Level		
	A=Excellent B=Good C=Fair D=Poor		
	Speaking	Listening	Writing
English			
Others__________			
Remarks			

Task 2 Translate the following positions into Chinese. Use dictionary if necessary.

1. human resources director ____________________
2. regional manager ____________________
3. quality control specialist ____________________
4. electrical technician ____________________
5. data analyst ____________________

6. technical engineer ____________________

7. general manager assistant ____________________

8. accountant ____________________

Task 3 Suppose you're looking for a job and the followings are positions you could apply for. Which one would you decide on? Why?

Job A: It's within walking distance of where you live, but the salary is lower than your expectation.

Job B: It provides an impressive salary but you have to work overtime quite often. And you need to move to a city that's unfamiliar to you.

Job C: It has flexible work time. The salary just meets your expectation, but you have no interest in the position at all and it's completely irrelevant to your major.

Task 4 Role Play

Imagine that you are having an interview. Please practice with your partner. One is the interviewer, and the other is the interviewee. Here are some possible questions and answers you may use:

Student A: Why are you interested in this position?/Why do you think you are capable of this job?/What do you think is your biggest strength?/What's your expected salary?/...

Student B: I'm interested in this job because.../I think I'm competent to do this work because.../My biggest strength is.../My expected salary is.../...

Unit 11

Part 6 Self-evaluation

评价项目	评价内容	自我诊断	改进措施
语言知识	I learn many common words and expressions about job hunting.	☐ Identifying ☐ Understanding ☐ Mastering	
认知能力	I know how to make a resume and prepare for an interview, and I come to realize what I value more about a job.	☐ Distinction ☐ Merit ☐ Pass ☐ Fail	
沟通能力	I can answer common questions in job interviews, and talk about the reasons for my choice of work in English.	☐ Distinction ☐ Merit ☐ Pass ☐ Fail	
文化意识	I get to learn about the creative job fair in China.	☐ Increasing ☐ Developing ☐ Weakening	

Part 7 Culture

Nighttime Job Fairs Offer Graduates More Options (Excerpt)

(from *https://www.chinadaily.com.cn*, Updated: 2023-09-04)

With nighttime activities, such as night markets, gaining more popularity among young people, many cities in China have leveraged these events to attract young job hunters.

In July, Yinzhou district in Ningbo, Zhejiang province, launched the "young talent night market", which was actually a huge nighttime job fair held for young people. Fifty local enterprises offered more than 700 job openings at the market.

The innovative employment fair attracted nearly 1,000 young job hunters.

"It's awesome that we can seek job opportunities while having a cup of coffee at the night market. It integrates nighttime activities that are popular among young people with important stuff such as finding a job," said He Yangwei, a college graduate from Taizhou, Zhejiang.

In addition to the job opportunities, the market also offered summer internships for college students.

"It's our creative attempt at a job fair. We hope that we can offer more opportunities and attract more young people by combining job hunting with recreation,"said Hu Dongping, deputy director of the Yinzhou district bureau of human resources and social security.

The night-market job fairs held in Haining, Zhejiang, in August attracted local employers as well as job seekers. At the market, young job seekers had the opportunity to speak with recruiters directly and leave their contact details for future communication.

Unlike the regular job fairs, which are held every Friday, the night-market job fairs are held on weekends and are targeted at college students, according to Haining's bureau of human resources and social security.

The markets are set up near high-traffic shopping malls, which allows young people to provide their resume when swinging by the mall.

Thanks to the digital employment platform "Intelligent Employment Code", job hunters no longer need to carry a printed resume. They can scan a code and fill in an application form on the platform if they find a matching job position at the markets.

Unit 12

Company

扫码看

Learning Objectives

After learning this unit, you should be able to:

1. get familiar with the words and expressions concerning company;
2. introduce the departments in companies, the history and products of a specific company and different levels of managers in English;
3. know that leadership skills and teamwork abilities are important.

Unit 12

Part 1 Topic Words and Expressions

扫码听

Departments in a Company

- office director
- Quality Inspection Department
- division
- Sales Department
- marketing
- Advertising Department
- affair
- cubicle
- Public Relations Department
- Human Resources Department
- Research and Development
- Department
- colleague
- hesitate

Company History and Products

- enter
- establish
- workforce
- employee
- growth
- engage
- design
- supplier
- globally

Managers in Organizations

- organization
- pyramid
- executive
- overall
- strategic
- oversee
- branch
- senior
- supervision
- section

Leadership Skills

- leadership
- decisiveness
- integrity
- collaborative
- individual
- resolution
- dependability
- mentor

Part 2 Lead-in

Wang Xia is taking her internship in a company. She gets familiar with the departments in the company, learns to introduce the history and products of the company and gets to know different levels of managers in an organization.

Part 3 Dialogs

Dialog 1 Departments in a Company

扫码听

(Wang Xia comes to the Quality Inspection Department for the first time.)

Wang Xia: Good morning. My name is Wang Xia. I'm here to see Mr. Johnson.

Mr. Johnson: Hello, I'm Stephan Johnson, the office director. Nice to meet you.

Wang Xia: Pleased to meet you, Mr. Johnson. I'm Wang Xia, from Huanghe Vocational College.

Mr. Johnson: Welcome to Quality Inspection Department. Let me show you around the office area first.

Wang Xia: Sure.

Mr. Johnson: There are many divisions here. This is the Sales Department and everyone here is responsible for selling products or services.

Wang Xia: What about marketing?

Mr. Johnson: The Advertising Department deals with marketing affairs. Let's move on.

Wang Xia: Would you mind telling me what's with the cubicles?

Mr. Johnson: This is the Public Relations Department, and they are responsible for contacts with other companies.

Wang Xia: I see. The Human Resources Department is over there.

Mr. Johnson: Yes, a place where hiring and firing happen. This is the Research and Development Department which we'll keep regular contact with.

Wang Xia: OK, I'll bear it in mind.

Mr. Johnson: Now we are at the Quality Inspection Department again.

Wang Xia: Shall I meet the colleagues?

Mr. Johnson: Sure. The guys here are very nice. If there is anything we can do for you, don't hesitate to ask. You'll adapt yourself to it in a couple of weeks.

Wang Xia: I do appreciate all you've done for me.

Notes

1. Let me show you around the office area first.
   我先带你在办公区转转。
2. Would you mind telling me what's with the cubicles?
   你能告诉我那些格子间是什么部门吗？
3. This is the Research and Development Department which we'll keep regular contact with.
   这里是研发部，我们会经常跟他们打交道。

Dialog 2 Company History and Products

扫码听

(Wang Xia is interested in the history and products of the company. She wants to get more information from Mr. Johnson.)

Wang Xia: I'm quite interested in the history and products of our company. Could you tell me something, Mr. Johnson?

Mr. Johnson: Sure. We started up in Shenzhen in 1986.

Wang Xia: It's nearly 40 years!

Mr. Johnson: You are right! In 1995, we entered the North American market and opened a sales office in New York.

Wang Xia: I know we have a European office.

Mr. Johnson: Yes. It was established three years later, in 1998. There are production centers in fifteen countries now.

Wang Xia: What about the workforce?

Mr. Johnson: Worldwide nearly 36,000 employees.

Wang Xia: Wow!

Mr. Johnson: That's because sales have gone up every year since we started. At one time they were doubling every month.

Wang Xia: Terrific! What's the main growth area now?

Mr. Johnson: Agricultural equipment. It is engaged in the design and production of all kinds of agricultural equipment.

Wang Xia: And our company is an excellent agricultural equipment supplier in the world.

Mr. Johnson: Absolutely! We are one of the leaders in this field globally.

Unit 12

Notes

1. That's because sales have gone up every year since we started.

   因为自公司成立起销售额逐年递增。

2. It is engaged in the design and production of all kinds of agricultural equipment.

   我们公司致力于设计和制造各种农业机械设备。

3. And our company is an excellent agricultural equipment supplier in the world.

   我们公司是世界上优秀的农业机械设备供应商。

Dialog 3 Managers in Organizations

扫码听

(Li Hua and Wang Xia are talking about the managers in organizations.)

Li Hua: I'm surfing the net to have a look at the pyramid structure of the managers in organizations.

Wang Xia: What's that?

Li Hua: In larger organizations, there're three levels of managers, top-level, middle-level, and lower-level managers.

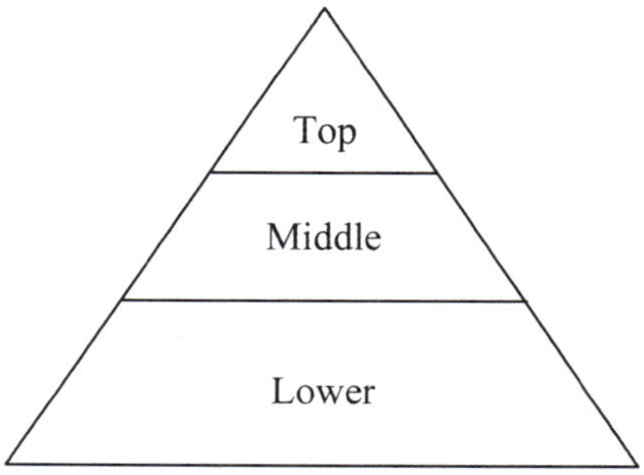

Wang Xia: I've only heard of C-level executives, like CEO, CFO, CTO, etc.

Li Hua: Yes, top-level managers consist of presidents and C-level executives.

Wang Xia: I know that they make decisions on the overall direction of the company, like company policies, strategic plans and so on.

Li Hua: They set a "tone at the top", and they are responsible for controlling and overseeing the operations of the entire company.

Wang Xia: Who are middle-level managers?

Li Hua: Middle-level managers include branch managers, regional managers, and department managers, etc.

Wang Xia: So they are between the front-line workers and top-level executives.

Li Hua: That's right! Middle-level managers communicate the strategic goals of senior management to the front-line managers.

Wang Xia: I guess the lower managers are responsible for basic supervision.

Li Hua: Yes, section leaders and team leaders are lower managers.

Notes

1. I know that they make decisions on the overall direction of the company, like company policies, strategic plans and so on.
   我知道他们决定公司的总体方向，比如公司政策、战略计划等。

2. Middle-level managers communicate the strategic goals of senior management to the front-line managers.
   中层管理人员将高层管理人员的战略目标传达给一线管理人员。
3. I guess the lower managers are responsible for basic supervision.
   我猜基层管理者负责日常监管。

Part 4 Passage

Six Top Skills of the Leadership

Almost any positive soft skill might be considered a leadership skill. For example, active listening helps leaders bring projects to completion by hearing the ideas and concerns of the team. Empathy, for example, helps leaders understand how their team feels about their workload, environment, and workplace relationships.

Here is a list of must-have leadership skills that may prove valuable to anyone applying for work or looking to advance in a career:

Decisiveness

Effective leaders are those who can make decisions quickly with the information they have. Effective decision-making comes with time and experience. As you become more familiar with your specific industry, you'll be able to make decisions faster, even when you don't have all the necessary information. Decisiveness is seen as a valuable leadership skill because it can help move projects along faster and improve efficiency.

Integrity

Integrity is often seen as just truthfulness or honesty, but, in many cases, it also means having and standing by a set of strong values. Integrity in the workplace often means being able to make ethical choices and helping the company maintain a positive image. All businesses seek to hire workers who have a strong sense of integrity.

Team building

Leadership requires the ability to build and maintain a strong and collaborative team of individuals working toward the same goal. Team building requires other leadership strengths, like effective communication skills and conflict resolution skills.

Problem solving

Good leaders are skilled at problem-solving issues that arise on the job. Effective problem solving often requires staying calm and identifying a step-by-step solution. Problem-solving skills can help leaders make quick decisions, resolve obstacles with their team and external teams alike, and ensure projects are completed on time, according to the specifications.

Dependability

Being a dependable leader means that people can trust and rely on you. A dependable person follows through on plans and keeps promises. The strong relationships built by a dependable leader create a resilient team that can work through difficulties that may arise.

Ability to teach and mentor

One of the skills that differentiates leadership from many other competencies is the ability to teach and mentor. Teaching colleagues effectively or directly reporting how to grow in their careers helps organizations scale. Often, this skill requires that leaders think less about themselves and more about how to make their team successful.

译文：六大领导技能

几乎所有积极的软技能都可以被视为领导技能。例如，积极倾听有助于领导者通过听取团队的想法和忧虑来促使项目完成。再如，同理心可以帮助领导者了解团队对其工作量、工作环境和职场人际关系方面的感受。

以下列出了一些可能对申请工作或寻求职业发展的人来说很有价值的必备领导技能：

决策能力

合格的领导者是可以利用所掌握的信息快速做出决策的人。高效的决策需要时间和经验。随着你对特定行业不断熟悉，即使没有所有必要的信息，也可以更快地做出决策。决策能力被认为是一项很宝贵的领导技能，因为它可以帮助我们加快项目进度，并提高效率。

诚信

诚信通常被视为坦率或者诚实。在许多情况下，诚信也意味着拥有并坚持一套强有力的价值观。职场诚信通常意味着能够做出合乎道德的选择，并帮助公司保持良好的形象。所有企业都寻求希望具有强烈诚信意识的员工。

团队建设

领导力要求有能力建立和维持一个强大而又协作的团队，以实现共同的目标。团队建设还需要其他的领导才能，例如，高效沟通技巧和解决冲突技巧。

解决问题

优秀的领导者善于解决工作中出现的问题。高效地解决问题，通常需要保持冷静，并制定分步解决方案。解决问题的技能，可以帮助领导者快速制定决策，与自己的团队及外部团队一道解决难题，并保质保量按时完成项目。

可靠性

成为可靠的领导者，意味着人们信任并依赖你。一个可靠的人，会贯彻计划并遵守诺言。由可靠的领导者建立的牢固关系，可以形成一支有韧性的团队，并能够克服可能出现的困难。

指导能力

领导能力与许多其他能力的一个不同之处是：指导能力。有效地教、指导同事或者直接告诉同事如何规划自己的职业发展，有利于组织的壮大。通常情况下，此技能要求领导者少考虑一些自己，更多去考虑如何让团队在整体上成功。

Part 5 Exercises

Task 1 Please translate the following expressions.

1. 广告部 ____________________
2. 公关部 ____________________
3. 人力资源部 ____________________
4. 销售部 ____________________
5. 研发部 ____________________
6. 质检部 ____________________
7. Production Department ____________________
8. Logistics Department ____________________
9. Customer Service Department ____________________
10. Manager Office ____________________

Task 2 The following short conversation is about the business operations of a company, but the sentences are completely disorganized. Put the sentences into proper order. Then practice the dialog with your classmate.

1	The growth's been unusual, then.
2	Digital cameras. They're really taking off.
3	What's the main growth area now?
4	The company started in 1986. At that time no one knew about our product, but now everyone seems to be using it.
5	That's right. Sales have gone up every year since we started. At one time they were doubling every month.
6	How long has your company been in business?

__________ → __________ → __________ → __________ → __________ → __________

Task 3 Please complete the sentences to list the responsibilities of managers.

1. Top-level managers are responsible for ________________________________.
2. Middle-level managers' tasks include ________________________________.
3. Lower-level managers provide ________________________________.

Task 4 Role Play

Student A: Imagine you are an intern of a company.

Please briefly introduce the company to others.

Student B: You are interested in the company.

Please ask student A for information about the company.

Change roles and try the role play again.

Part 6 Self-evaluation

评价项目	评价内容	自我诊断	改进措施
语言知识	I learn many common words and expressions about company.	☐ Identifying ☐ Understanding ☐ Mastering	
认知能力	I know the different levels of managers in companies and their responsibilities.	☐ Distinction ☐ Merit ☐ Pass ☐ Fail	
沟通能力	I can use English to ask for and provide information about company history and products.	☐ Distinction ☐ Merit ☐ Pass ☐ Fail	
文化意识	I get to learn about dedication and sacrifice in positions.	☐ Increasing ☐ Developing ☐ Weakening	

Unit 12

Part 7 Culture

Huawei to Roll Out 5.5G Equipment (Excerpt)

(from *http://www.chinadaily.com.cn*, Updated: 2023-07-20)

Huawei Technologies Co., Ltd will launch a complete set of commercial 5.5G network equipment next year, as part of a broader push to speed up the evolution of 5G and kick off the 5.5G era for the information and communications technology industry.

The plan comes amid rapid progress in 5G deployment over the past four years that is already yielding significant financial gains, experts said, adding that the fast-approaching 5.5G will be a key milestone in 5G evolution.

Huawei proposed the concept of a "5.5G Era" to protect telecom operators' investment in 5G, and improve network performance by 10 times.

Huawei has been working with multiple players across the industry on R&D and verification of key 5.5G technologies, with significant progress, specifically in extremely large antenna arrays which underpin 10-gigabit downlinks, flexible spectrum access that helps in realizing gigabit uplinks, and passive IoT that can enable 100 billion IoT connections.

According to the company, 50G PON is another key technology that can enable 10-gigabit speeds for F5.5G ultra-broadband networks, and is expected to be extensively used in homes, campuses, and industry in the future.

Huawei has worked with over 30 operators around the world on technological verification and application pilots for these technologies, the company said.

The industry is still in its earliest stage of developing a vision for 6G, and has only just begun related research into key technologies. This is the reason why many have turned to 5.5G as their milestone for future development. The 10-fold improvement in network capabilities in the 5.5G era is set to enable numerous industries to unleash the productivity of digital technology, Huawei said.

Unit 13

Office English

扫码看

Learning Objectives

After learning this unit, you should be able to:

1. get familiar with the words and expressions concerning office English;
2. know how to communicate with your workmates as an intern in English;
3. know that Chinese software industry has been greatly developed.

Unit 13

Part 1 Topic Words and Expressions

扫码听

Report for Duty

- duty
- intern
- hand over
- opposite
- work-issued
- Logistics Department
- corridor

First Task

- enviable
- seriously
- proficient
- seminar
- nameplate
- attendee
- version
- specification
- format

Task Accomplished

- accomplish
- expectation
- modify
- enlarge
- font
- bold
- effect
- modification
- definitely
- wireless
- wired
- driver
- install

Printer Installation Guide for Windows

- rear
- capable
- wizard
- router
- Ethernet
- panel
- plug
- application
- device
- right-click
- property
- pop-up
- congratulation

Part 2 Lead-in

It's time for Wang Xia to execute her specific tasks as an intern in ABC Company. Her trainer, Zhang Jia, is waiting to help her.

Part 3 Dialogs

Dialog 1 Report for Duty

扫码听

(Wang Xia goes to her office to find her trainer.)

Wang Xia: Excuse me, is Miss Zhang Jia in? Mr. Johnson asked me to report for my duty to her.

Zhang Jia: Oh, I'm Zhang Jia. You must be the new intern today, right?

Wang Xia: Yes, my name is Wang Xia.

Zhang Jia: OK! I've been waiting for you. It's glad to see you.

Wang Xia: Pleased to meet you, Miss Zhang.

Zhang Jia: Fine. Mr. Johnson has handed over your internship to me. I'll help you to get familiar with your work.

Wang Xia: Thank you very much, Miss Zhang.

Unit 13

Zhang Jia: Come on. The opposite desk is yours now and that is your work-issued laptop.

Wang Xia: Thanks a lot!

Zhang Jia: Never mind. And here is your power-on password. You'd better change it after entering the system.

Wang Xia: Okay, I've got it.

Zhang Jia: Remember to go to the Logistics Department to get the office supplies you need. When you complete your internship, the computer should be returned to the company.

Wang Xia: All right. Can you tell me how to get to the Logistics Department, Miss Zhang?

Zhang Jia: Well, no problem. Turn right after leaving this office, and you'll find it at the end of the corridor on this floor. Got it?

Wang Xia: Yes, I'll keep that in mind.

Notes

1. Mr. Johnson asked me to report for my duty to her.
   是约翰逊先生让我来找她报到的。
2. Mr. Johnson has handed over your internship to me.
   约翰逊先生让我带你实习。
3. You'll find it at the end of the corridor on this floor.
   它就在这层走廊的尽头。

Dialog 2 First Task

(After organizing her desk, Wang Xia comes to seek for her assignment.)

扫码听

Wang Xia: I'm prepared, Miss Zhang. Is there anything I can do next? I want to get familiar with the job as soon as possible.

Zhang Jia: OK, let's get down to business. Here is the first assignment for you. I heard you are proficient in using office software?

Wang Xia: Yeah, I've learned a lot in college, especially WPS.

Zhang Jia: That's great. There will be a seminar at 12: 00 this afternoon, with leaders of other branches. We should make some nameplates for the attendees in advance to arrange the meeting place. Please make an electronic version of the nameplates first and bring it to me for checking. If there's no problem, print it out.

Wang Xia: No problem. Where can I get the name list? And are there any specifications for the size and format?

Zhang Jia: Do you have a DingTalk account?

Wang Xia: Yes, of course. I also have joined the company group as required.

Zhang Jia: Good. Then I'll transfer a document to you through DingTalk. You can find everything you need in it.

Wang Xia: OK!

Zhang Jia: You are welcome.

Notes

1. Let's get down to business.

说正事儿吧。

2. I have joined the company group as required.

我已经按要求加入公司群了。

Unit 13

Dialog 3 Task Accomplished

扫码听

(Wang Xia has completed her task and gives a feedback to Zhang Jia.)

Wang Xia: Are you available now, Miss Zhang?

Zhang Jia: Just a minute. I need to save this document first.

(A few moments later)

Zhang Jia: So, what's the problem?

Wang Xia: Er... I've sent the electronic file I have made to you with expectations for your advice.

Zhang Jia: Wow. Already accomplished? You're so proficient!

Wang Xia: I did some similar work in the student union before. It just came in handy.

Zhang Jia: OK, I'll view it at once.

Wang Xia: Please tell me if there is anything necessary to be modified.

Zhang Jia: Well, nothing serious. But I suggest you enlarge the font size to 130 pt and make it bold.

Wang Xia: Good idea! The effect will be better and clear in this way! I'll modify it immediately.

Zhang Jia: Then you can print the nameplates out after your modification.

Wang Xia: OK. Which printer should I use?

Zhang Jia: The one against the wall. Remember to use red printing paper over there.

Wang Xia: Definitely! Is it wireless or wired?

Zhang Jia: Both are OK. The drivers are already installed.

Wang Xia: Great. But I haven't used this brand of printer before.

Zhang Jia: Take it easy. The printers are almost the same in use. And the instructions are on the machine anyway.

Wang Xia: That sounds good. Let me have a try.

(Wang Xia have printed the nameplates and brings them to Zhang Jia.)

Wang Xia: Here are the printed nameplates for you, Miss Zhang.

Zhang Jia: Well done! Just in time. Let's go to arrange the meeting place!

Notes

1. Are you available now?

你现在有空吗?

2. It just came in handy.

刚好派上用场。

3. I suggest you enlarge the font size to 130 pt and make it bold.

建议你把字号放大到 130 磅并加粗。

Part 4 Passage

Printer Installation Guide for Windows

Are you preparing to install your printer on your computer but don't know how to install it? Here is an installation guide for you.

Step 1: Connect your printer to your computer.

There are three methods that you can connect your printer to your computer.

Method 1: USB connection to your computer

Unit 13

You can connect your printer with a USB cable.

(1) Turn on your computer and your printer.

(2) Use a USB cable to connect the USB port on the rear of your printer and your computer.

Method 2: Wireless (Wi-Fi) connection to your computer (a wireless-capable printer is needed)

If your printer is wireless-capable, you can connect your printer to your network with the guided Wireless Setup Wizard on the printer.

(1) Turn on your printer, router, and computer.

(2) Remove any USB or Ethernet cables from your printer.

(3) Make sure your computer is connected to the same wireless network you are connecting the printer to.

(4) On your printer control panel, go to the "Setup" "Network" or "Wireless" menu, and then open "Wireless Setup Wizard" to follow the on-screen instructions to connect the printer to your network.

Method 3: Wired connection to your computer

You can also connect your printer and your computer to your router with a standard Ethernet cable.

(1) Turn on your printer.

(2) Remove any plug from the Ethernet port (the port with the 品 logo) on the rear of your printer.

(3) Use the Ethernet cable to connect the printer port and an available port on

your router.

Step 2: Install the printer driver for your printer.

Insert your printer driver CD that came with your printer and run the printer setup application (usually “setup.exe”) to install the driver for your printer.

If you lose your printer driver CD, don’t worry. You can download the driver from the official website based on your printer model.

Step 3: Print test paper

Now, you can print test paper to check whether your printer works or not.

(1) On your keyboard, press the Windows logo key and R at the same time to open the Run dialog, then type “control” and press “Enter” on your keyboard to open the Control Panel.

(2) Click Devices and Printers to view your printer.

(3) Right-click your printer and select “Printer Properties”.

(4) In the pop-up window, click “Printer Test Page”.

If a test paper is printed, congratulations! You’ve set up your printer.

译文：适用于 Windows 的打印机安装指南

您是否准备在计算机上安装打印机，但不知道该如何做？以下是提供给您的安装指南。

步骤 1：将打印机连接到计算机上。

有三种方法可以将打印机连接到计算机上。

方法 1：使用 USB 连接打印机到您的计算机。

您可以用 USB 数据线连接您的打印机：

（1）请打开您的电脑和打印机。

（2）使用 USB 数据线将打印机和计算机后部的 USB 端口连接到一起。

方法 2：使用无线（Wi-Fi）连接打印机到您的计算机（需要使用具有无线功能的打印机）

如果您的打印机具有无线功能，那么您可以通过打印机上的无线安装向导程序来将打印机连接到网络上。

（1）请打开打印机、路由器和电脑。

（2）请将所有 USB 数据线或以太网电缆从您的打印机上移除。

（3）确保您的计算机连接的无线网络与打印机将要连接的无线网络相同。

（4）在打印机控制面板上，进入“安装”“网络”或“无线”菜单，然后打开“无线安装向导”，按照屏幕上的说明将打印机连接到网络。

方法 3：使用电缆连接打印机到您的计算机。

您还可以用一根标准的以太网电缆将打印机和计算机连接到路由器上。

（1）打开你的打印机。

（2）将打印机后部以太网端口（带有 品 标识的端口）中的插头移除。

（3）使用以太网电缆连接打印机端口和路由器上的一个可用端口。

步骤 2：为打印机安装驱动程序

插入打印机附带的打印机驱动程序光盘，并运行打印机安装应用程序（通常是“setup.exe”）来为打印机安装驱动程序。

如果你的打印机驱动程序光盘丢失，不用担心，你可以根据你的打印机型号从官方网站下载该驱动程序。

步骤 3：打印测试页

现在，您可以打印测试页来检查您的打印机是否已经可以工作。

（1）在键盘上同时按下 Windows 标志的开始菜单键和 R 键，打开“运行”对话框，在对话框中输入“control”并按“Enter”键，打开控制面板。

（2）单击“设备和打印机”以查看您的打印机。

（3）鼠标右键单击您的打印机，并选择“打印机属性”。

（4）在弹出的窗口中，单击“打印机测试页面”。

如果测试页打印成功，那么恭喜您，您已经设置好您的打印机了！

Part 5 Exercises

Task 1 Look at the following company map. Suppose you are an intern at the reception. Please try to tell the visitor how to find the conference hall.

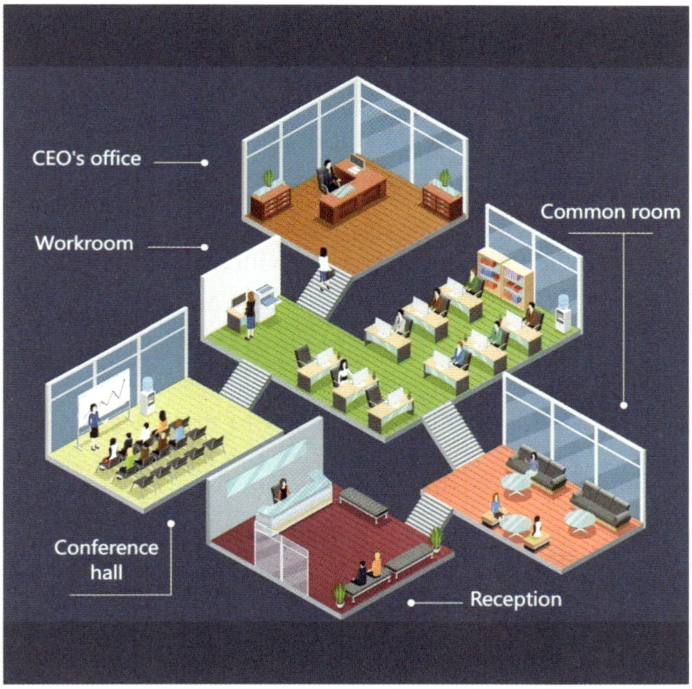

Task 2 This instruction is on a printer of your office. Some of its text is missing. Please complete it with the words below.

clean	paper	off	button	pull

How to use a printer

- Step 1: Press the green (1) ________.
- Step 2: Put in the (2) ________.
- Step 3: Click print.

Unit 13

How to deal with possible problems

◆ Jams

Turn off your printer first, then carefully (3) ________ out the paper.

◆ Overheating

Turn it (4) ________ for 15 minutes before turning it on again.

◆ What else to know

Regularly (5) ________ the printer and its other parts.

Task 3 Please match the English expressions with the icons.

1. Align Right	A. 
2. Italic Font	B. 
3. Bold Font	C. 
4. Open	D. 
5. Align Left	E. **B**
6. Print Preview	F. ***I***
7. Align Both Ends	G. 
8. Save	H. 
9. Print	I. 
10. Center	J. 

Task 4 Role Play

Student A: Imagine you are an intern in the ABC Company.

Ask your trainer about how to fulfil your assignments.

Student B: Imagine you are the trainer of an intern.

Answer the intern's questions and assign some tasks to him/her.

Change roles and try the role-play again.

Unit 13

Part 6 Self-evaluation

评价项目	评价内容	自我诊断	改进措施
语言知识	I learn many common words and expressions about office English.	☐ Identifying ☐ Understanding ☐ Mastering	
认知能力	I know how to discuss work assignments with workmates.	☐ Distinction ☐ Merit ☐ Pass ☐ Fail	
沟通能力	I can use office English to communicate with my workmates.	☐ Distinction ☐ Merit ☐ Pass ☐ Fail	
文化意识	I get to learn about great achievements in Chinese software industry.	☐ Increasing ☐ Developing ☐ Weakening	

Part 7 Culture

China's Software Industry Accelerates Innovation and Resilience Over Past Decade (Excerpt)

(from *https://global.chinadaily.com.cn,* Updated: 2022-05-02)

China's software industry has accelerated innovation and strengthened resilience over the past decade, *People's Daily* reported on Wednesday.

The revenue of the country's software industry grew from about 2.5 trillion yuan ($370 billion) to about 9.5 trillion yuan with an annual growth rate of 16.1 percent from 2012 to 2021.

The innovation capability of China's software industry has increased significantly in the past decade with a number of software practitioners growing from 4.7 million to 8.09 million between 2013 and 2021.

In the same period, China's intellectual property protection has made impressive progress and in return created well protected innovations. The number of computer software copyright registrations increased from 139,200 in 2012 to 2.28 million in 2021.

The country has promoted application of software over the past decade. By the end of last year, the digital control rate of key processes in industrial enterprises and

the penetration rate of digital R&D and design tools reached 55.3 and 74.7 percent respectively.

The gap between the maturity of domestic and international mainstream products has been narrowed significantly. These products include operating systems, databases and basic software such as office software.

Harmony OS, or Hongmeng in Chinese, Huawei's open-source operating system, has been cumulatively installed in more than 240 million devices, and WPS office software products cover more than 220 countries and regions.

The performance of domestic 3D CAD (computer-aided design) products has approached the international middle level and the market share of domestic business management industrial software has reached 70 percent.

Alibaba Cloud Computing has cumulatively served 900 million Chinese people and over 4 million corporate customers worldwide with the strong support of the Apsara operating system.

China is expected to significantly improve the supply capacity of key software such as basic software and industrial software and build 2 to 3 open-source communities with international influence by 2025, according to a development plan of China's software and information technology service industry from 2021 to 2025.

Unit 14

Schedule, Appointment and Reception

扫码看

Learning Objectives

After learning this unit, you should be able to:

1. get familiar with the words and expressions concerning schedule, appointment, and reception;
2. learn to report the schedule to the superior, make appointments and receive guests;
3. know that appropriate behavior is important in workplace.

Unit 14

Part 1 Topic Words and Expressions

扫码听

Reporting the Schedule

- arrangement
- negotiate
- attach
- preparation
- candidate
- assistant
- post
- participate
- quality
- regard
- remind
- importer
- add

Making an Appointment

- receive
- at the moment
- introduce
- further
- cooperation
- check
- break
- note

Reception

- meeting room
- mind
- take a seat
- terribly
- emergency
- biscuits

Why is Office Etiquette so Important?

- etiquette
- considerate
- mindful
- chronically
- punctuality
- gossip
- reputation
- cooperative

Part 2 Lead-in

Li Hua and Wang Xia are interning at different posts in ABC Company. They learn to report schedule to the superior, make appointments and receive guests.

Part 3 Dialogs

Dialog 1 Reporting the Schedule

(Li Hua reports to Ms. Song, the sales manager, on the arrangements of the next day.)

扫码听

Li Hua: Ms. Song, I've worked out your schedule of tomorrow. Would you like to take a look at it?

Ms. Song: Just read it out to me.

Li Hua: At 9:30 in the morning, you'll be meeting with the production manager of XYZ Company to negotiate pricing.

Ms. Song: XYZ Company has developed rapidly in recent years and has become one of our major customers. Do attach great attention to the preparation.

Li Hua: I see. Then from 1:30 to 3:00 p.m., you'll be interviewing the applicants of sales assistants. As far as I know, there are nearly 20 candidates for the 4 posts.

Ms. Song: Maybe you can participate in the interview with me. Pay attention to their communication skills. High EQ is an indispensable quality for sales assistants.

Li Hua: Sure. Then at 3: 30 p.m., you'll be attending a middle-level manager meeting regarding the launch of our new product line. And the Vice President will attend the meeting.

Ms. Song: OK. Remember to remind me at 3: 10 p.m. Which meeting room?

Li Hua: Room 103. Finally, at 7: 00 p.m., you'll be having dinner with an important importer from Canada.

Ms. Song: All right. Anything else?

Li Hua: Nothing. Is there anything you'd like to add regarding the schedule?

Ms. Song: No. That's OK.

Notes

1. XYZ Company has developed rapidly in recent years and has become one of our major customers.

   XYZ 公司近年来发展迅速，已成为我们的主要客户之一。

2. Pay attention to their communication skills. High EQ is an indispensable quality for sales assistants.

   注意他们的沟通技巧。高情商是销售助理不可或缺的品质。

3. Then at 3: 30 p.m., you'll be attending a middle-level manager meeting regarding the launch of our new product line.

   下午 3: 30，你将参加一个中层经理会议，主题是关于新产品线投产。

Dialog 2 Making an Appointment

扫码听

(Li Hua, the assistant of Ms. Song, receives a telephone call from Jason Smith of XYZ Company.)

Li Hua: Hello, this is ABC Company. What can I do for you?

Jason Smith: Hi, this is Jason Smith of XYZ Company. May I speak to Ms. Song?

Li Hua: Sorry, I'm afraid Ms. Song is not in at the moment.

Jason Smith: Then can you make an appointment for me? I'd like to have a talk to Ms. Song to introduce our new product, and see if we can have further cooperation.

Li Hua: Yes, of course. Let me check her schedule and see if I can arrange it for you.

Jason Smith: Thank you.

Li Hua: Er... Ms. Song might be available on Wednesday morning and Thursday afternoon.

Jason Smith: Well, could I make an appointment at Thursday afternoon, please?

Li Hua: Let me see... In that case, would 3: 30 be convenient? Ms. Song has a one-hour break from 3: 30 to 4: 30.

Jason Smith: Yes, that's fine.

Li Hua: I'll take a note of that. Would you like me to confirm your appointment?

Jason Smith: Yes, please. 3: 30 to 4: 30 on Thursday afternoon, right?

Li Hua: That's right. Shall I take a message for you?

Jason Smith: Sure, Jason Smith from XYZ Company would like to see Ms. Song to talk about the new product and further cooperation.

Li Hua: Got it! See you then!

Jason Smith: Thanks! See you.

Unit 14

Notes

1. I'm afraid Ms. Song is not in at the moment.
   恐怕宋女士现在不在。
2. Let me check her schedule and see if I can arrange it for you.
   我查一下她的日程安排，看看能不能帮你安排一下。
3. Ms. Song might be available on Wednesday morning and Thursday afternoon.
   宋女士可能在星期三上午和星期四下午有空。

Dialog 3 Reception

扫码听

(Wang Xia works at the front desk this week. Jason Smith from XYZ Company comes to visit Ms. Song at 3 : 15 this afternoon.)

Wang Xia: Good afternoon, Sir. What can I do for you?

Jason Smith: Good afternoon. My name is Jason Smith and I work for XYZ Company. I have an appointment with Ms. Song at 3 : 30.

(Wang Xia checks the schedule.)

Wang Xia: Yes, Ms. Song will see you at the meeting room. This way, please. Mind the steps.

Jason Smith: Thank you.

(At the meeting room)

Wang Xia: Please take a seat, Mr. Smith, and do you want anything to drink? Coffee, tea, or water?

Jason Smith: Thanks, water will be fine.

Wang Xia: My pleasure, cold or warm?

Jason Smith: Cold, please.

Wang Xia: Just a moment.

(Wang Xia prepares cold water and hands the water to Jason Smith.)

Wang Xia: Here you are.

(Wang Xia receives a phone call from Li Hua, the assistant of Ms. Song.)

Wang Xia: Mr. Smith, I am terribly sorry Ms. Song is caught in some emergency and maybe need another 10 minutes.

Jason Smith: Em…

Wang Xia: Would you like some biscuits?

Jason Smith: No, thanks.

Wang Xia: Er, Mr. Smith, would you like to take a look at our office? It would be my pleasure to show you around.

Jason Smith: All right.

Notes

1. I have an appointment with Ms. Song at 3: 30.

   我和宋女士约好 3: 30 见面。

2. Mr. Smith, I am terribly sorry Ms. Song is caught in some emergency and maybe need another 10 minutes.

   史密斯先生，非常抱歉，宋女士现在有点急事，可能还需要十分钟。

3. It would be my pleasure to show you around.

   我非常乐意带您参观。

Part 4 Passage

Why is Office Etiquette so Important?

With good office etiquette, everyone can be comfortable and effective in the workplace.

Unit 14

What is good office etiquette? Simply speaking, having good office etiquette means that you are respectful and considerate both of your co-workers and of the overall office environment around you.

Here are a few cautions we think you should be especially mindful of on workplace etiquette.

Noise

Usually, talking too loudly or too much are the problems. Talking too loudly or discussing personal affairs over the phone is not appropriate for a workplace environment.

Timeliness

Just show up on time. If you're a person who's chronically late, you'll be seen as someone who doesn't take their job responsibilities seriously. Also, it's important to remember that punctuality is about respecting other people's time, as well as your own.

Gossiping

Gossip can sometimes be seen as a form of currency in offices because people feel special or privileged if they feel they know something that others don't, but this kind of behavior just leads to infighting among co-workers. So it's best to avoid gossip.

Office events

In short, you should always try to attend them. Of course, missing out every once in a while is certainly fine but you don't want to develop a reputation as somebody who's always too important or too busy to participate in office events. Overall, you want to be seen as a team player within your office.

Common use spaces

The biggest issue of common use spaces is usually the question of overall cleanliness. Let's start here by talking about the office break room. In short, keep things clean. If you make a mess, clean it up. It's that simple.

Of course, you're not perfect and neither is anyone else and it's unreasonable to expect perfection from anyone including yourself. However, if there is someone in your workplace who's consistently breaking the rules of good office etiquette, it can lead to a demoralized and unproductive workplace and it should be dealt with. So the simplest way in these kinds of situations is to keep calm and rational and handle it in private if you can help it.

In conclusion, if you follow all the advice we've put forward here today, you should hopefully be seen by your co-workers and your superiors as someone who's cooperative and a valued member of the company.

译文：为什么办公室礼仪如此重要？

有了良好的办公室礼仪，每个人在工作场所都能感到舒适和高效。

什么是良好的办公室礼仪？简单地说，良好的办公室礼仪意味着你对同事和周围的整个办公室环境都很尊重和体贴。

在办公室礼仪方面，以下是一些我们认为您应该特别注意的事项。

噪声

通常，这里的问题是说话太大声或太多。在工作场所大声说话或在电话中讨论私事，是不合适的。

准时

要守时。如果你是一个长期迟到的人，你会被视为一个不认真对待工作职责的人。此外，重要的是要记住，守时就是尊重他人的时间，也尊重自己的时间。

闲谈

流言蜚语有时可以被视为办公室里的一种货币，因为如果人们觉得自己知道别人不知道的事情，就会感到特别或有特权，但这种行为只会导致同事之间的内讧。所以最好避免流言蜚语。

办公室活动

简而言之，你应该尽量参加。当然，偶尔错过一次当然没关系，但你不想成为一个总是太重要或太忙而无法参加办公室活动的人。总的来说，你希望在办公室里被视为一个团队成员。

公用空间

公用空间最大的问题通常是整体清洁度的问题。让我们从办公室休息室开始。简而言之，保持清洁。如果你弄得一团糟，就把它清理干净，就这么简单。

当然，你并不完美，其他人也不完美，期望包括你自己在内的任何人都完美是不合理的。然而，如果你的工作场所中有人一直违反良好的办公室礼仪规则，这可能会导致工作场所士气低落，效率低下，应该加以处理。因此，在这种情况下，最简单的方法是保持冷静理智，如果你能帮忙的话，个人私下处理。

总之，如果遵循了我们今天在这里提出的所有建议，你应该有望被同事和上级视为一个有合作精神的人，并被视作公司的重要成员。

Part 5 Exercises

Task 1 Please make a timetable for Ms. Song according to Dialogue 1.

Time	Arrangements

Task 2 Please write the words of a week according to the abbreviations. The first one has already been done for you as an example.

MON. ____Monday____ TUE. ________________

WED. ________________ THU. ________________

FRI. ________________ SAT. ________________

SUN. ________________

Task 3 Can you find alternatives for the following sentences according to the context of dialog 3?

1. What can I do for you?

____.

2. This way, please.

____.

3. Mind the steps.

____.

4. Please take a seat.

____.

5. Do you want anything to drink?

____.

6. Just a moment.

____.

7. Would you like some biscuits?

____.

8. Would you like to take a look at our office?

____.

9. It would be my pleasure to show you around.

____.

10. All right.

____.

Task 4 Role Play

Student A: Imagine you are Mr. Lee, a manager.

Ask questions about your schedule of a business trip.

Student B: Imagine you are the secretary of Mr. Lee.

Answer the questions of Mr. Lee and report the arrangement of the trip.

Change roles and try the role play again.

Part 6 Self-evaluation

评价项目	评价内容	自我诊断	改进措施
语言知识	I learn many common words and expressions about schedule, appointment, and reception.	☐ Identifying ☐ Understanding ☐ Mastering	
认知能力	I know the language of reporting schedules, making appointment, and receiving guests.	☐ Distinction ☐ Merit ☐ Pass ☐ Fail	
沟通能力	I can receive guests appropriately.	☐ Distinction ☐ Merit ☐ Pass ☐ Fail	
文化意识	I get to learn about the importance of good language and proper behavior.	☐ Increasing ☐ Developing ☐ Weakening	

Unit 14

Part 7 Culture

Tencent Unveils Large Language Model (Excerpt)

(form *https://www.chinadaily.com.cn*, Updated: 2023-09-08)

Tencent Holdings, a leading homegrown technology company, debuted its much-awaited universal large language model Hunyuan on Thursday, as Chinese enterprises strive to gain a foothold in the global artificial intelligence race.

Hunyuan has a scale of over 100 billion parameters and pre-training data of over 2 trillion tokens, two standards used to measure the power of AI models, said Dowson Tong, senior executive vice-president of Tencent.

Hunyuan can support a wide array of functions, including creating content and images, text recognition and generating relevant meeting minutes, Tong said at the Tencent Global Digital Ecosystem Summit on Thursday.

The latest model has, he said, been already connected to more than 50 of Tencent's own products and services, such as WeChat search, cloud, advertising, gaming, financial technology, online meeting and documents.

With Tencent the latest to join the list, nearly all leading Chinese internet companies, including Baidu, Alibaba Group, JD and ByteDance, have jumped on the AI-powered LLM bandwagon. By July-end, there were more than 130 LLMs in China and "a new era of a hundred models has begun", said Jiang Jie, Tencent's vice-president, at the summit.

He said Hunyuan was better than OpenAI's GPT-4 in areas such as writing lengthy Chinese text and solving certain math problems.

Last month, Beijing granted the first batch of approvals for generative AI services and gave the green light to eight technology firms, including AI firm SenseTime Group, to offer ChatGPT-like chatbots to the public.

As the global AI race becomes increasingly fierce, Chinese companies should continue to strengthen investment and research in AI for self-reliance, said Liu Dian, a senior researcher at the China Institute of Fudan University.

Unit 15

Career Planning and Lifelong Learning

扫码看

Learning Objectives

After learning this unit, you should be able to:

1. get familiar with the words and expressions concerning career planning, lifelong learning, and ways of continuing education;
2. introduce one's career plan, the concepts and ways of lifelong learning in English;
3. know that lifelong learning is essential to everyone and popular in China.

Unit 15

Part 1 Topic Words and Expressions

扫码听

Career Planning

- training
- graduation
- assessment
- easy-going
- academic
- foundation
- preparatory
- assistant controller
- contact

Lifelong Learning

- lifelong learning
- sign up
- pre-school
- post-retirement
- senior citizen
- refer to
- undertake
- qualification
- frequently
- challenge
- constant
- adapt

Different Ways of Continuing Education

- continue
- product tester
- superior
- confusion
- wonder
- specialized
- distance learning
- forum
- take… into account

Change of Career Paths Brings Challenges and Rewards

- reward
- opt to
- pursue
- financial
- access
- diversified
- emerge
- sociology
- tolerance
- livestreaming

Part 2 Lead-in

Before finishing his internship in ABC Company, Li Hua talked to his superior about his future career plan. Li Hua and Wang Xia get to know the concepts of lifelong learning. While Li Na who has been working as a product tester for one year is talking to her superior about her plan of further education.

Part 3 Dialogs

Dialog 1 Career Planning

扫码听

(Li Hua is talking to Ms. Song about his future plan.)

Ms. Song: Congratulations, Li Hua. You are about to finish your internship in ABC Company. You did a great job!

Li Hua: Thanks, Ms. Song. I've learned a lot here. Practical training is the last course of my college life. I tried my best to put what I've learned into practice. I know I still have a long way to go.

Ms. Song: Do you have any plan after graduation?

Li Hua: Yes, I have made my mind to work in the accounting field since I entered the college, because I took a course called Career Planning when I was a freshman. The teacher told us to set goals according to self-assessment, our interests, and majors.

Unit 15

Ms. Song: From the personality point of view, you are quiet, independent, and easy-going. Your high sense of responsibility is a necessary quality to accountants. More importantly, you major in accounting.

Li Hua: Yeah. Besides, I like reading books and work hard in order to build a strong academic foundation for future career.

Ms. Song: You have showed that to all of us!

Li Hua: I have applied for a position of accountant in XYZ Company and I hope in 3 to 4 years, I can get both working experience and an MBA or Master's degree in accounting.

Ms. Song: Good idea! Everybody spends the first 3 to 4 years in the career in a preparatory position.

Li Hua: I hope in 6-7 years, I can become an assistant controller in a mid-to large-sized company.

Ms. Song: Then I have a suggestion that you'd better take your first job in a large corporation that can bring you important practical experience and a broad network of contacts.

Li Hua: I'll keep that in mind.

Ms. Song: Besides, it's important to make your superiors aware of your goal and persuade them to support your career goal by providing you with opportunities.

Li Hua: Thank you, Ms. Song.

Notes

1. The teacher told us to set goals according to self-assessment, our interests, and majors.
   老师告诉我们要根据自我评估、兴趣和专业来设定目标。
2. I have applied for a position of accountant in XYZ Company and I hope in 3 to 4 years,

I can get both working experience and an MBA or Master's degree in accounting.
我已经申请了 XYZ 公司的会计职位，我希望在 3 到 4 年内，我能获得工作经验的同时取得 MBA 或会计硕士学位。

3. Then I have a suggestion that you'd better take your first job in a large corporation that can bring you important practical experience and a broad network of contacts.
那么我建议你第一份工作最好找一家大公司，它能给你带来重要的实践经验和广泛的人脉。

Dialog 2 Lifelong Learning

(Li Hua signed up for an MBA course. He mentioned lifelong learning when talking with Wang Xia.)

扫码听

Wang Xia: Why did you enroll the MBA course?

Li Hua: Everybody is learning from pre-school kids to post-retirement senior citizens. Lifelong learning is so popular!

Wang Xia: That's true. Some people engage in degree course at university, some people acquire vocational skills at the workplace and even parents learn to use AI from their children.

Li Hua: Everybody is learning at all stages of life, such as taking part in sports, cultural activities, and volunteer activities. Lifelong learning refers to all learning activities undertaken throughout life, in order to acquire abilities, knowledge and qualifications.

Wang Xia: I agree that we can always learn something new from everywhere and everybody.

Li Hua: Lifelong learning becomes more important because the world keeps changing fast.

Unit 15

Wang Xia: Yeah, nowadays, one probably does not take the same job until retirement, but changes jobs frequently, so he or she needs new skills and knowledge to meet new challenges.

Li Hua: Constant learning can make us more learned and experienced so that we can catch up with the changing world.

Wang Xia: Even people who don't plan to change their jobs need to learn in order to adapt to social and economic life.

Li Hua: Learning can keep our minds active.

Wang Xia: I agree with you.

Notes

1. Some people engage in degree course at university, some people acquire vocational skills at the workplace and even parents learn to use AI from their children.
   有的人在大学学习学位课程，有的人在工作场所习得职业技能，甚至父母向孩子学习使用人工智能。
2. Lifelong learning refers to all learning activities undertaken throughout life, in order to acquire abilities, knowledge and qualifications.
   终身学习是指在一生中为获得能力、知识和资格证书而进行的所有学习活动。

Dialog 3 Different Ways of Continuing Education

扫码听

(Li Na has been working as a product tester for one year. She is talking to her superior, Mr. Blade, about her plan of further education.)

Li Na: It's my honor to have a talk with you, Mr. Blade.

Mr. Blade: The face-to-face regular communication is also a good chance for me to know your expectations for future, your ideas to the job or any problems, if you have.

Li Na: I do have a confusion as to the future learning, Mr. Blade. You know, I've been on the position of product test for 1 year. I found that I have a lot to learn, so I wonder if I can engage in advanced studies.

Mr. Blade: That's a good idea. It's never too old to learn. I'm sure you know exactly what you need now.

Li Na: Yes, I urgently need specialized knowledge of pneumatic circuit, but I have no idea how to do that.

Mr. Blade: Nowadays there're different ways of learning, such as visiting the local library to read trade journals, registering online courses, and taking part in distance learning of the universities. It is not necessary to be getting a new degree, if you long to acquire knowledge, abilities, or skills you need.

Li Na: Yes, you reminded me that there're also forums of machinery which introduce professional knowledge and the latest developments in our industry.

Mr. Blade: Those are valuable resources. You can make a "to-learn" list. Write down all the points you want to learn and finish them one by one.

Li Na: Thanks for your suggestion, Mr. Blade. I'm full of confidence that I can take both work and learning into account.

Mr. Blade: Good luck!

Unit 15

Notes

1. The face-to-face regular communication is also a good chance for me to know your expectations for future, your ideas to the job or any problems, if you have.
定期面对面交流也是我了解你对未来的期望、对工作的想法或任何问题（如果有的话）的好机会。

2. Nowadays there're different ways of learning, such as visiting the local library to read trade journals, registering online courses, and taking part in distance learning of the universities.
现在有不同的学习方式，比如去本地图书馆阅读行业期刊、注册在线课程、参加大学的远程学习等。
3. You reminded me that there're also forums of machinery which introduce professional knowledge and the latest developments in our industry.
你提醒了我，还有一些机械行业论坛介绍专业知识和我们行业的最新发展情况。

Part 4 Passage

Change of Career Paths Brings Challenges and Rewards

Many workers, especially the young, are opting to leave the traditional job market to pursue more flexible employment opportunities.

Su Lan, a human resources director worked in Hangzhou, Zhejiang province, said: "Young people nowadays have less financial pressure than those born in the 1970s and 1980s, as they grow up in a more open-minded society with more access to information. As a result, they have greater freedom to make their own decisions."

As employees' attitudes toward work change, along with increasingly diversified employment methods in different industries, new forms of flexible employment are emerging.

Workers want flexibility in where, when and how they are employed. Since 2019, there has been an 83 percent rise in the number of job posts mentioning "flexibility", according to LinkedIn's *Global Talent Trends Report* issued in January. On individual companies' LinkedIn profiles, references to "flexibility" in posts rose by 343 percent over the same period.

Yu Hai, a sociology professor at Fudan University in Shanghai, said, "Traditional forms of employment have diversified in these fast-changing times, while society is showing greater tolerance for newly emerging occupations."

According to latest data from the National Bureau of Statistics, by the end of 2022, the number of workers in flexible employment in China reached 200 million—more than 1.6 million of them in livestreaming and other forms of new media, nearly a threefold year-on-year rise.

译文：职业的改变带来挑战和回报

许多人，尤其是年轻人，选择离开传统的就业市场，寻求更灵活的就业机会。

在浙江省杭州市工作的人力资源总监苏兰说：“现在的年轻人比 20 世纪七八十年代出生的人经济压力更小，因为他们在一个更开放、更容易获得信息的社会中长大。因此，他们有更大的自由做出自己的决定。”

随着员工对工作态度的转变，以及不同行业的就业方式越来越多样化，新的灵活就业形式正在出现。

工人们希望在工作地点、时间和方式上有灵活性。根据领英 1 月份发布的《全球人才趋势报告》，自 2019 年以来，提及“灵活性”的职位数量增加了 83%。在个别公司的领英个人资料中，帖子中提到的“灵活性”同期增加了 343%。

上海复旦大学社会学教授于海说：“在这个快速变化的时代，传统的就业形式已经多样化，而社会对新兴职业表现出了更大的宽容。”

根据国家统计局的最新数据，截至 2022 年年底，中国灵活就业人数达到 2 亿，其中 160 多万人从事直播和其他形式的新媒体运营，人数同比增长了近三倍。

Part 5 Exercises

Task 1 Please fill in the form below according to dialogue 1.

My Career Plan		
Self-assessment	Personality	
	Major	
	Interest	
My goal		
Ways to achieve my goal		

Task 2 Please translate the following quotes about learning into Chinese.

1. When you know a thing, to recognize that you know it; and when you do not know a thing, to recognize that you do not know it—that is wisdom.

    ____

2. It's never too old to learn.

    ____

3. Achievement is founded on diligence and wasted upon recklessness.

    ____

4. Our life has a limit but knowledge has none.

    ____

5. A young idler, an old beggar.

    ____

Task 3 In order to avoid repetition, multiple expressions are commonly used in English even though they have similar meanings. Please try to find out alternatives for the following phrases or sentence patterns in dialogue 3.

1. continuing education ____________________
2. product tester ____________________
3. I did have a confusion as to… ____________________
4. engage in ____________________
5. specialized knowledge ____________________

Task 4 Role Play

Student A: Imagine you are a teacher.

Ask questions about career plan of Student B

Student B: You are a college student.

Answer the teacher's questions and report your career planning.

Change roles and try the role play again.

Part 6 Self-evaluation

评价项目	评价内容	自我诊断	改进措施
语言知识	I learn many common words and expressions about career planning, lifelong learning, and ways of continuing education.	☐ Identifying ☐ Understanding ☐ Mastering	
认知能力	I know the steps of career planning.	☐ Distinction ☐ Merit ☐ Pass ☐ Fail	
沟通能力	I can introduce the concepts and ways of lifelong learning in English.	☐ Distinction ☐ Merit ☐ Pass ☐ Fail	
文化意识	I get to know that lifelong learning is essential to everyone and popular in China.	☐ Increasing ☐ Developing ☐ Weakening	

Unit 15

Part 7 Culture

Bluebook Calls for Smarter Education (Excerpt)

(from *https://global.chinadaily.com.cn*, Updated: 2023-02-15)

As China moves toward a modern country with a strong education sector, smart education must see greater growth, according to a new bluebook.

Digital technologies are the bedrock for smart education, which features diverse data application and sharing, and calls for the collective creation and sharing of digital education resources and a renewed commitment to a global community of smart education, said the China Smart Education Bluebook 2022.

The bluebook was released by the China National Academy of Educational Sciences during the World Digital Education Conference, which was held in Beijing from Monday to Tuesday.

As digital technologies integrate deeper into education, countries will be able to draw on each other's strengths, allowing smart education to benefit all, the bluebook said.

More efforts are needed to integrate new technologies seamlessly into teaching to meet the needs of learners. The use of technologies, facilities and devices should not be the sole focus in the efforts to create a smart learning environment, and improving teaching methods and practices is also important, it said.

The bluebook suggested including smart education in the broader agenda of China's transition to a digital and smart society.

Keys to Tasks

Unit 1 Campus Life

Keys to Part 5:

Task 1: 1. stretch 2. lecture 3. notice board 4. regret 5. canteen

Task 2: get some stretches and build up body

train logic and improve communication skills

promote reading and writing skills

cultivate innovative thinking

enhance hands-on ability

Task 3: 略

Task 4: 略

Unit 2 Learning in College

Keys to Part 5:

Task 1: 1. C 2. E 3. D 4. A 5. B

Task 2: Xiao Qi: Appreciation of Dramas

Jay Wang: Introduction to Psychology

Tan Fei: Basketball Tactics

Teresa Liu: Chinese Calligraphy

Li Qing: Mathematical Modeling Method

Task 3: how to fill in the accounting voucher

to register various detailed accounts

check accounts with each other

Task 4: 略

Unit 3 Shopping

Keys to Part 5:

Task 1: 1. H 2. E 3. J 4. A 5. F 6. G 7. C 8. D 9. B 10. I

Task 2: 1. help 2. take 3. storeroom 4. try 5. price

Task 3: 1. 我想把这双鞋退了。

2. 我可以退款吗?

3. 我想把这条裙子换个别的颜色。

4. 我可以看一下您的收据吗?

5. 您来得真及时，今天刚好是 7 天无理由退货的最后一天。

Task 4: 略

Unit 4 Food

Keys to Part 5:

Task 1: 1. E 2. F 3. G 4. H 5. C 6. D 7. A 8. B

Task 2: 1. 麻婆豆腐

2. 回锅肉

3. 宫保鸡丁

4. 夫妻肺片

Task 3: 1. reservation 2. Under

3. menu 4. order

5. Dutch 6. bill

Task 4: 略

Unit 5 Friends and Families

Keys to Part 5:

Task 1: 1. daughter 2. uncle 3. nephew 4. father-in-law 5. sister-in-law
6. wife 7. bridegroom

Task 2: 1. 新娘 2. 新郎 3. 哥哥 4. 妹妹
5. 姐（妹）夫；内弟（兄）；小叔；大伯
6. 婆婆；岳母
7. 侄子；外甥
8. 侄女；外甥女
9. 兄弟姐妹
10. 祖父母；外祖父母

Task 3: 1. 患难见真情。
2. 人生在世无朋友，犹如生活无阳光。
3. 父亲是财富，兄弟是安慰，朋友兼而有之。
4. 天下无不散之筵席。/ 送君千里终须一别。
5. 好书如挚友，情谊永不渝。

Task 4: 略

Unit 6 Health

Keys to Part 5:

Task 1: 1. headache
2. stomachache
3. cough
4. fever
5. sneeze

6. toothache

Task 2: A, E, B, D, G, C, F

Task 3: 略

Task 4: 略

Unit 7 Public Transport

Keys to Part 5:

Task 1: 2, 4, 3, 1

Task 2: Log in; destination; the travel date; the passenger; payment

Task 3: First, they can take Line 4 to go to Xizhimen Station, then transfer to Line 2 to Gulou Dajie Station, and transfer to Line 8 to the destination.

Task 4: 略

Unit 8 Travelling

Keys to Part 5:

Task 1: 1. kettle 2. sheet 3. reception 4. toilet paper 5. faucet 6. hair dryer 7. bolt 8. socket

Task 2: 1. 我订了房间，想办理入住。

2. 我们的卫生纸用完了，你能送点过来吗？

3. 能再给我一个枕头吗？

4. 洗手间里没有肥皂。

5. 我想退房。

Task 3: 略

Task 4: 略

Unit 9 Customs of Chinese Festivals

Keys to Part 5:

Task 1: 1. The Double Ninth Festival / The Chongyang Festival

2. The Lantern Festival / The Yuanxiao Festival

3. The Dragon Boat Festival / The Duanwu Festival

Task 2: 1. honor

2. absorb

3. suggested

4. suitable

5. stomach

Task 3: 1. True

2. False (Qingming Festival is usually around the fifth day of the fourth solar month.)

3. False (People are accustomed to appreciating chrysanthemums on the Double Ninth Festival.)

4. True

5. True

Task 4: 略

Unit 10 China's Achievements

Keys to Part 5:

Task 1: 3, 4, 2, 1

Task 2: T, F, T, F, T

Task 3: was launched, manned spacecraft, spaceflight, space station, spacewalks

Task 4: 略

Keys to Tasks

Unit 11 Job Hunting

Keys to Part 5:

Task 1: Example of an application form.

Employment Application Form

Position of Interest					
Position	Translation	Expected Salary	¥6,500		(Photo)
Personal Information					
Name	Zhang Hong	Gender	☐ Male ☑ Female		
Nationality	Chinese	Place of Birth	Jinan, Shandong Province		
Date of Birth (MM/DD/YY)	2/12/2000	Age	23		
ID Type	☐ Passport ☐ ID Card ☐ Exit & Entry Permit		ID Number	××××××××××××××	
Email	Zhanghong@×××.com		Mobile Number	(+86) 156××××××××	
Residential Address	××× Road, Jinan, Shandong Province				

Educational Background					
Education & Training	Name of School	From MM/YY To MM/YY	Major Studies	Certificate	Status
University/ College	××× University	From 09/2019 To 06/2023	Translation	Bachelor of Arts	☑ Completed ☐ Not Completed ☐ In Progress
High School	×××High School	From 09/2016 To 06/2019			☑ Completed ☐ Not Completed ☐ In Progress
Others					☐ Completed ☐ Not Completed ☐ In Progress

Working History				
Are you currently employed?	☐ Yes ☑ No			
Working Period	From (M) (Y) To (M) (Y)			
Company		Telephone Number		
Title				
Job Responsibilities				

Professional Skills
Translation Certificate

Language Skills			
Language	Level		
	A=Excellent B=Good C=Fair D=Poor		
	Speaking	Listening	Writing
English	A	A	A
Others________			
Remarks			

Task 2: 1. 人事主管 / 主任；2. 地区经理；3. 质量控制专员；4. 电气技术员；5. 数据分析员；6. 技术工程师；7. 总经理助理；8. 会计

Task 3: 略

Task 4: 略

Keys to Tasks

Unit 12　Company

Keys to Part 5:

Task 1: 1. Advertising Department

2. Public Relations Department
3. Human Resources Department
4. Sales Department
5. Research and Development Department
6. Quality Inspection Department
7. 生产部
8. 后勤部
9. 客服部
10. 经理办公室

Task 2: 6, 4, 3, 2, 1, 5

Task 3: 1. making decisions on the overall direction of the company

2. communicating the strategic goals of senior management to the front-line managers
3. basic supervision

Task 4: 略

Unit 13　Office English

Keys to Part 5:

Task 1: Please go upstairs to the common room first, and up the left staircase to the workroom. Go straight and there's a printer against the wall. Then step down the stair on the left, you'll find the conference room.

Task 2: (1) button

(2) paper

(3) pull

(4) off

(5) clean

Task 3: 1. I　2. F　3. E　4. A　5. G　6. D　7. J　8. C　9. B　10. H

Task 4: 略

Unit 14　Schedule, Appointment and Reception

Keys to Part 5:

Task 1:

Time	Arrangements
9: 0 a.m.	meeting with the production manager of XYZ Company to negotiate pricing
1: 00-3: 00 p.m.	interviewing the applicants of sales assistants
3: 30 p.m.	attending a middle-level manager meeting regarding the launch of our new product line
7: 00 p.m.	having dinner with an important importer from Canada

Task 2: Monday　Tuesday　Wednesday　Thursday　Friday　Saturday　Sunday

Task 3: 1. Can I help you?

2. Please follow me.

3. Watch your step.

4. Sit down, please.

5. Would you like a drink? / Something to drink? / What would you like to drink?

6. Wait a minute.

7. Do you want some biscuits?

8. Why don't you take a look at the office?

9. I feel honored to be your guide.

10. OK.

Task 4: 略

Unit 15 Career Planning and Lifelong Learning

Keys to Part 5:

Task 1:

My Career Plan		
Self-assessment	Personality	quiet, independent, easy-going, high sense of responsibility
	Major	accounting
	Interest	reading books
My goal	● to work in the accounting field ● in 3 to 4 years: a position of accountant ● in 6-7 years: become an assistant controller in a mid- to large-sized company.	
Ways to achieve my goal	● study hard in order to build a strong academic foundation ● get working experience in first 3-4 years ● get an MBA or Master's degree in accounting ● take my first job in a large corporation ● make my superiors aware of my goal and persuade them to support me by providing me with opportunities	

Task 2: 1. 知之为知之，不知为不知，是知也。

2. 活到老，学到老。

3. 业精于勤，荒于嬉。

4. 吾生也有涯，而知也无涯。

5. 少壮不努力，老大徒伤悲。

Task 3: 1. further education, future learning, advanced studies

2. (people) on the position of product test

3. I have no idea…

4. take part in

5. professional knowledge

Task 4: 略

Appendix 1

International Phonetic Alphabet

国际音标

音标（International Phonetic Symbol），是记录音素的符号，也是音素的标写符号。英语音标中有元音20个，辅音28个，共48个。

英语音标汇总表

元音	单元音	长元音	/ɑː/	/ɔː/	/ɜː/	/iː/	/uː/		
		短元音	/ʌ/	/ɒ/	/ə/	/ɪ/	/ʊ/	/e/	/æ/
	双元音	/eɪ/	/aɪ/	/ɔɪ/	/əʊ/	/aʊ/	/ɪə/	/eə/	/ʊə/
辅音	爆破音	/p/	/t/	/k/			清辅音		
		/b/	/d/	/g/			浊辅音		
	摩擦音	/f/	/θ/	/s/	/ʃ/	/h/	清辅音		
		/v/	/ð/	/z/	/ʒ/	/r/	浊辅音		
	破擦音	/tʃ/	/ts/	/tr/			清辅音		
		/dʒ/	/dz/	/dr/			浊辅音		
	鼻　音	/m/	/n/	/ŋ/			浊辅音		
	半元音	/w/	/j/				浊辅音		
	舌侧音	/l/					浊辅音		

Appendix 1

元音 Vowel

元音（Vowel），又称母音，是音素的一种，与辅音相对。元音是在发音过程中气流通过口腔而不受阻碍发出的音。发元音时，气流从肺中压出，经过气管进入口腔，通过声门冲击声带，使声带发出均匀震动，然后震音气流不受阻碍地通过口腔，通过舌、唇的调节而发出不同的声音。舌的前后、高低，唇的圆扁，都会影响从肺中出来的气流，使之发出不同的元音。

英语元音共有20个，其中单元音12个，双元音8个。

单元音发音规则

/ʌ/	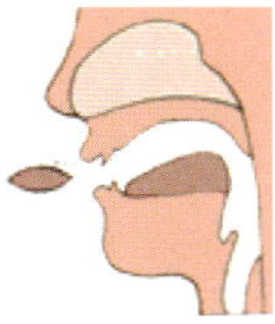	短元音	舌中部向上腭抬起，舌端离开下齿，舌身自然平展；唇形放松、扁平；极为短促的气流从口腔中冲出，振动声带，发出此音
/ɑ:/	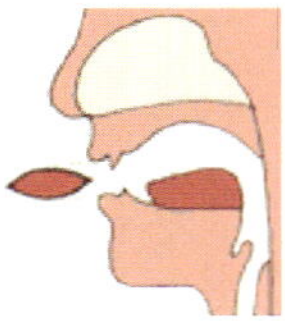	长元音	舌端离开下齿，舌身平放后缩，舌位较低；口张大，口形自然缩成圆形；气流从口腔中流出，振动声带，发出此音
/ɒ/	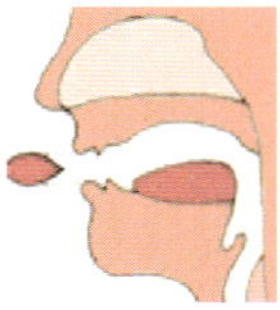	短元音	舌尖离开下齿，舌身尽量降低并后缩；双唇自然成圆形，嘴角有紧绷的感觉，保持口形不变；一股极为短促的气流从口腔中冲出，振动声带，发出此音
/ɔ:/	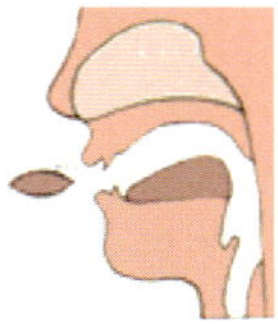	长元音	舌尖离开下齿，舌后抬高，上下唇略为张大，唇形较圆，并用力向前突出；气流从口腔中冲出，振动声带，发出此音

/ə/	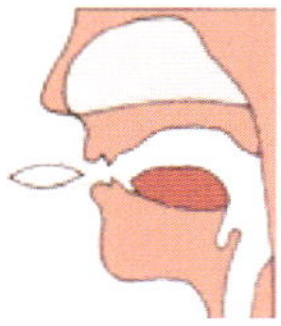	短元音	舌端离开下齿，舌身平展而放松，舌中部向上腭抬起；双唇略扁，使嘴微张，舌尖靠近下齿龈，但不贴紧；气流从口腔中冲出，微振声带，发出此音
/ɜː/	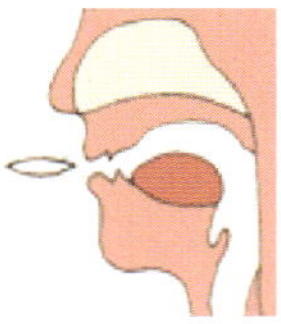	长元音	舌端离开下齿，舌身平展，舌中部稍微抬起；双唇扁平，向左右略微拉开；气流从口腔中冲出，微振声带，发出此音
/ɪ/	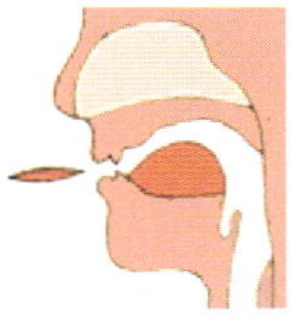	短元音	舌尖轻抵下齿龈，舌前部向硬腭抬起；嘴角向后缩使双唇略扁；极为短促的气流从口腔中冲出，微振声带，发出此音
/iː/	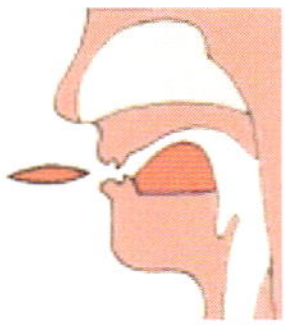	长元音	舌尖轻抵下齿龈，舌前部抬高，但不抵上齿龈；嘴角向后缩，使双唇呈扁平状；气流从口腔中流出，振动声带，发出此音
/ʊ/	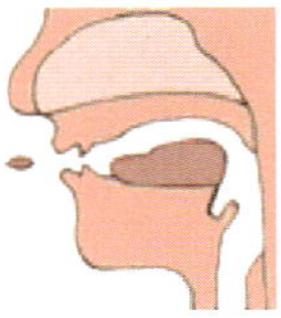	短元音	舌端离开下齿，舌后部向软腭抬起；双唇圆而小，稍向前突出；极为短促的气流从口腔中冲出，振动声带，发出此音
/uː/	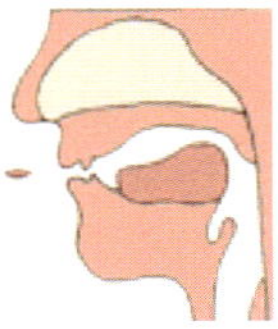	长元音	舌端离开下齿，舌后部向软腭抬高，舌位明显高于/ʊ/音；双唇尽量收缩成圆而小，小于/ʊ/的唇形，并稍向前突出；气流从口腔中冲出，振动声带，发出此音
/e/	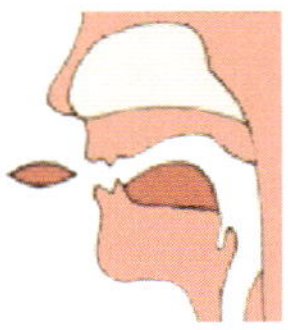	短元音	舌端靠近下齿，舌前部稍稍抬起；双唇扁平，上下齿的距离相当于一个中指宽度；极为短促的气流从口腔中冲出，振动声带，发出此音

/æ/	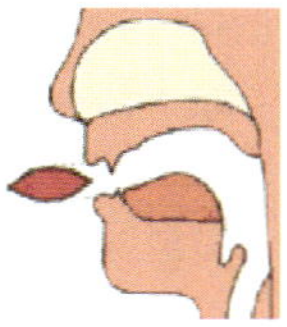	短元音	舌端靠近下齿，舌前部向硬腭抬起的程度比 /e/ 低；双唇尽量向两边平伸，使嘴角肌肉感到紧张，上下齿的距离相当于两个中指宽度；极为短促的气流从口腔中冲出，振动声带，发出此音

双元音发音规则

/eɪ/	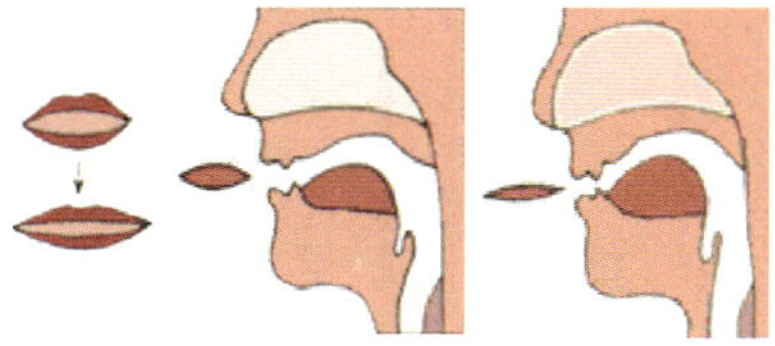	口形由 /e/ 向 /ɪ/ 的舌位滑动，/e/ 发得清楚响亮，/ɪ/ 发得模糊短促；唇形扁平，舌位由到高低；气流从口腔中冲出，振动声带，发出此音
/aɪ/	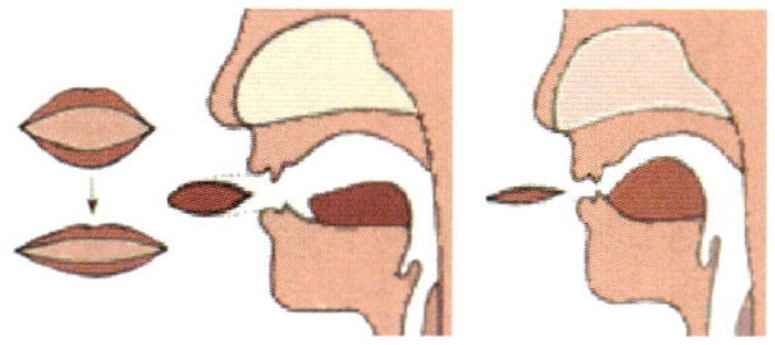	口形由 /a/ 向 /ɪ/ 的舌位滑动，/a/ 发得清楚响亮，/ɪ/ 发得模糊短促；唇形扁平，由大到小，舌位由低到高；气流从口腔中冲出，振动声带，发出此音
/ɔɪ/	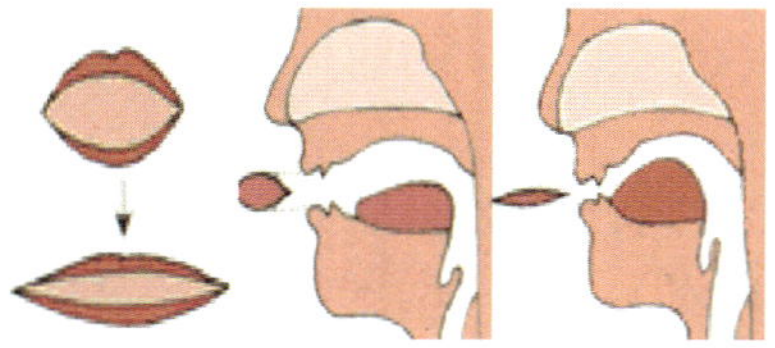	口形由 /ɔ/ 向 /ɪ/ 的舌位滑动，/ɔ/ 发得清楚响亮，/ɪ/ 发得模糊短促；唇形由圆形变成扁平，舌位由低到高；气流从口腔中冲出，振动声带，发出此音
/əʊ/	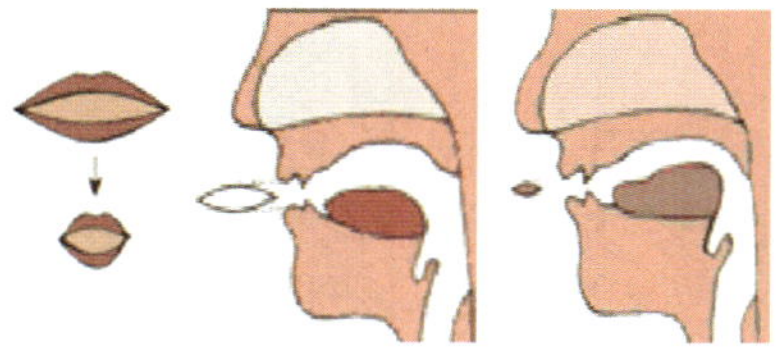	口形由 /ə/ 向 /ʊ/ 的舌位滑动，/ə/ 发得响亮，/ʊ/ 发得模糊短促；唇形从扁平到略圆，舌位由低到高；气流从口腔中冲出，振动声带，发出此音
/aʊ/	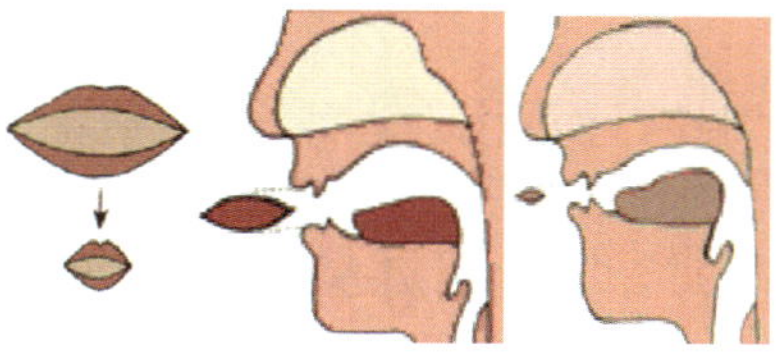	口形由 /a/ 滑向 /ʊ/，/a/ 发得响亮，/ʊ/ 发得短促；唇形由扁平到圆形，由小到大，舌位由低到高；气流从口腔中冲出，振动声带，发出此音

/ɪə/	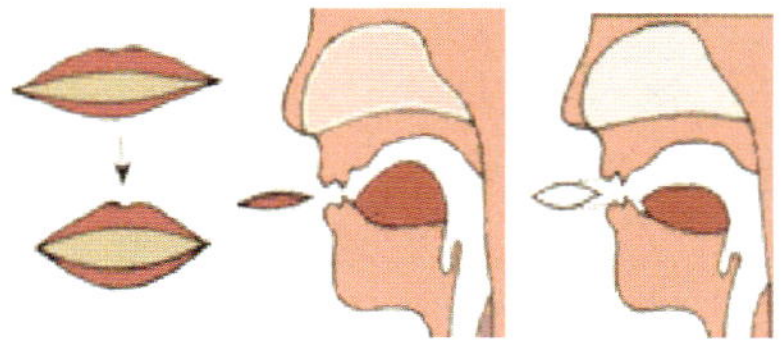	口形由 /ɪ/ 很快滑向 /ə/，/ɪ/ 发得清楚响亮，/ə/ 发得短促；唇形由扁平到自然，舌位由高到低；气流从口腔中冲出，振动声带，发出此音
/eə/	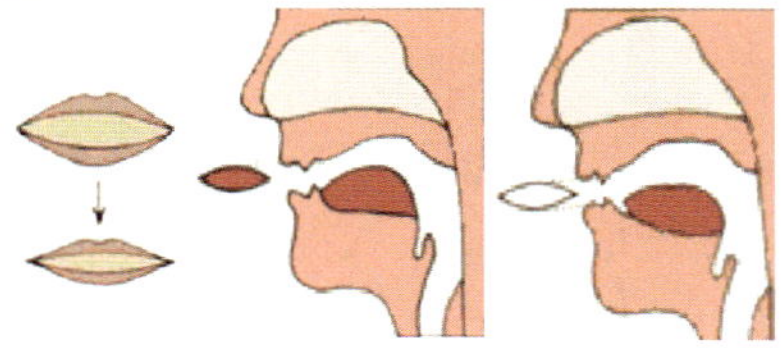	口形由 /e/ 很快滑向 /ə/，发 /e/ 时舌尖靠近下齿，唇形由扁平到自然，舌位由低到高；气流从口腔中冲出，振动声带，发出此音
/ʊə/	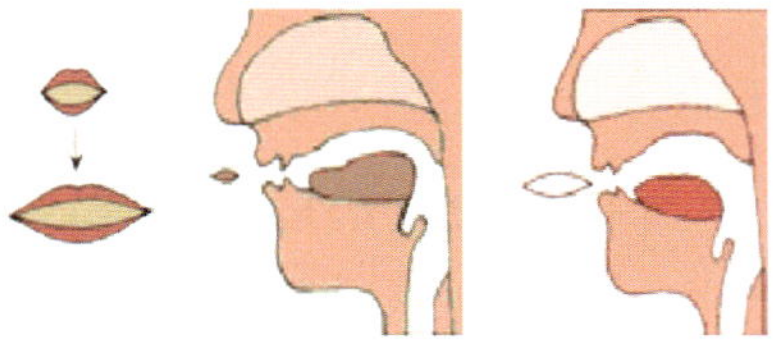	由 /ʊ/ 很快滑向 /ə/，/ʊ/ 发得清晰响亮，/ə/ 发得短促；唇形由圆形到扁平，舌位由高到低；气流从口腔中冲出，振动声带，发出此音

辅音 Consonant

辅音（Consonant），又叫子音，是指发音时气流受到发音器官的各种阻碍而形成的音。发音时声带不一定振动，音素不够清晰响亮。发音时声带振动的是浊辅音，声带不振动的是清辅音。

爆破音发音规则

/p/	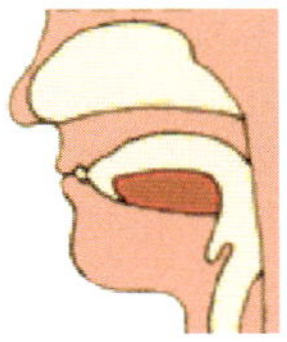	清辅音	舌身自然平放在口腔中，双唇紧闭，在口腔内形成一股气流；气流由双唇迸出，不振动声带，发出此音
/b/	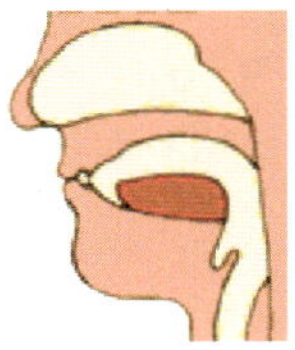	浊辅音	舌身自然平放在口腔中，双唇紧闭，在口腔内形成一股气流；气流由双唇迸出，振动声带，发出此音

Appendix 1

/t/	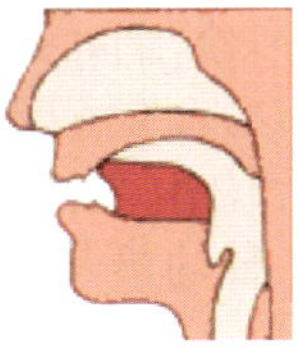	清辅音	舌尖轻抵上齿龈，嘴微张；舌与硬腭之间聚集一股气流；气流由舌尖和上齿龈之间冲出，同时，舌尖迅速离开上齿龈，不振动声带，发出此音
/d/	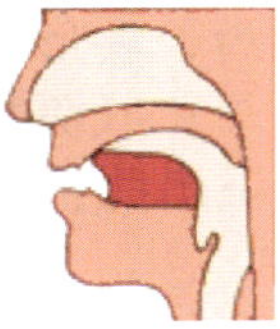	浊辅音	舌尖轻抵上齿龈，嘴微张；舌与硬腭之间聚集一股气流；气流由舌尖和上齿龈之间冲出，同时，舌尖迅速离开上齿龈，振动声带，发出此音
/k/	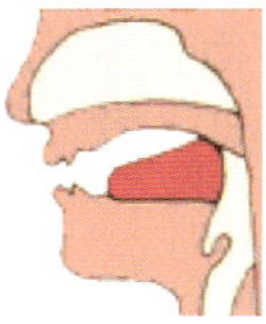	清辅音	舌后部抬高并使其紧贴软腭，嘴微张；舌后部与软腭之间聚集一股气流；气流由舌后部和软腭之间冲出，同时，舌后部与软腭迅速分离，不振动声带，发出此音
/g/	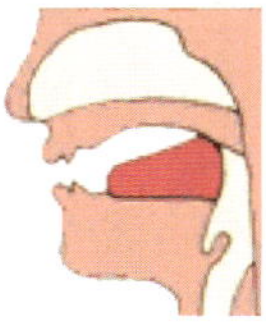	浊辅音	舌后部抬高并使其紧贴软腭，嘴微张；舌后部与软腭之间聚集一股气流；气流由舌后部和软腭之间冲出，同时，舌后部与软腭迅速分离，振动声带，发出此音

摩擦音发音规则

/f/	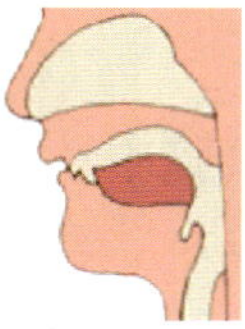	清辅音	上齿轻触下唇；气流从唇与齿之间的空隙泄出，产生一定摩擦；不振动声带，发出此音
/v/	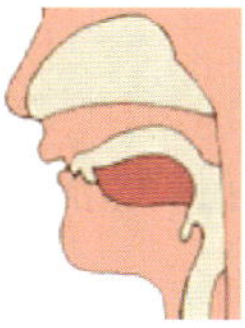	浊辅音	上齿轻触下唇；气流从唇与齿之间的空隙泄出，产生一定摩擦；振动声带，发出此音

/θ/	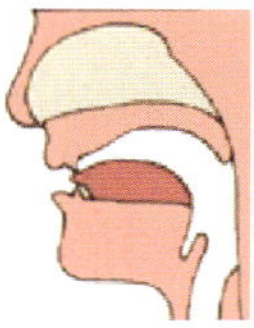	清辅音	将舌尖略微伸出，放在上下齿之间，使舌尖两面轻触上下齿；气流从舌和齿间流出，但口腔内各部位保持不动；不振动声带，发出此音
/ð/	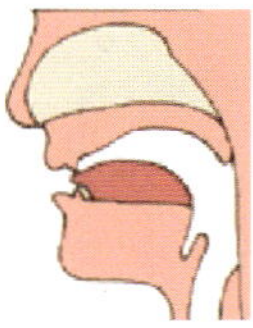	浊辅音	将舌尖略微伸出，放在上下齿之间，使舌尖两面轻触上下齿；气流从舌和齿间流出，但口腔内各部位保持不动；振动声带，发出此音
/s/	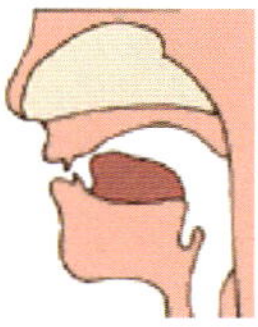	清辅音	舌尖接近上齿龈，舌尖与上齿龈之间的距离较小；气流从舌头与硬腭和齿龈之间摩擦而出；不振动声带，发出此音
/z/	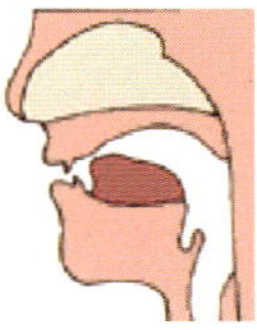	浊辅音	舌尖接近上齿龈，舌尖与上齿龈之间的距离较小；气流从舌尖与齿龈之间狭缝中摩擦而出，吐气较弱；振动声带，发出此音
/ʃ/	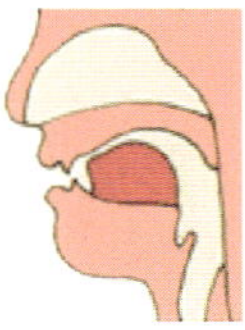	清辅音	舌叶接近上齿龈后部与硬腭前部，双唇略突出；气流从舌身与硬腭前部之间，通过齿龈和舌尖之间流出；不振动声带，发出此音
/ʒ/	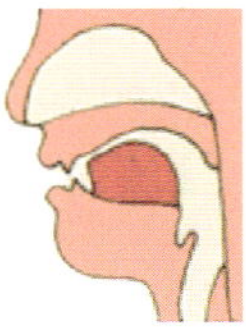	浊辅音	舌叶接近上齿龈后部与硬腭前部，双唇略突出；气流从舌身与硬腭前部之间，通过齿龈和舌尖之间流出；振动声带，发出此音
/h/	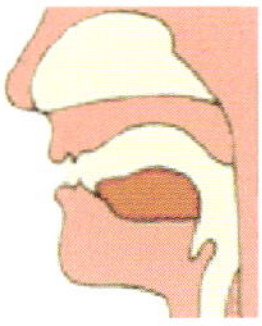	清辅音	双唇张开，舌身平放于口腔中，并使其保持轻松状态；气流通过声门时发生轻微摩擦，然后从口腔泄出；不振动声带，发出此音

/r/	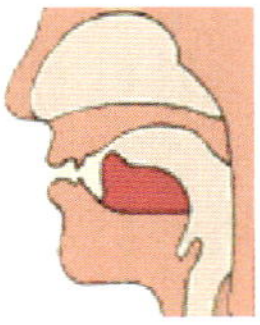	浊辅音	将舌尖卷起，停在口腔中央，不贴住口腔任何部位；双唇稍微向外突出，不要太用力；气流由舌面和硬腭之间流出，振动声带，发出此音

破擦音发音规则

/tʃ/	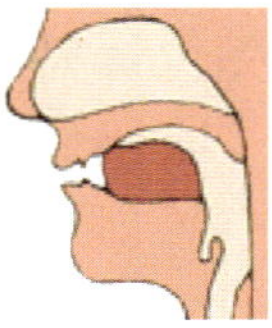	清辅音	舌尖抵住上齿龈，形成发 /t/ 的音位，然后舌尖与上齿慢慢分开，让气流从它们之间的狭缝中摩擦而出；唇形从 /ʃ/ 的自然张开过渡到略微突出的唇形；不振动声带，发出此音
/dʒ/	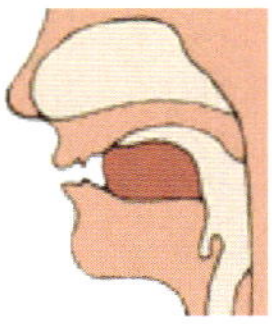	浊辅音	舌尖抵住上齿龈，形成发 /d/ 的音位，然后舌尖与上齿慢慢分开，让气流从它们之间的狭缝中摩擦而出；唇形从 /ʒ/ 的自然张开过渡到略微突出的唇形；振动声带，发出此音
/ts/	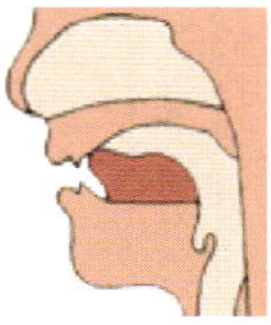	清辅音	舌端抵住上齿龈，形成阻碍；舌端略下降，气流随即冲出口腔，摩擦成音；不振动声带，发出此音
/dz/	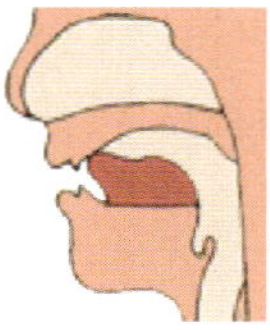	浊辅音	舌端抵住上齿龈，形成阻碍；舌端略下降，气流随即冲出口腔，摩擦成音；振动声带，发出此音
/tr/	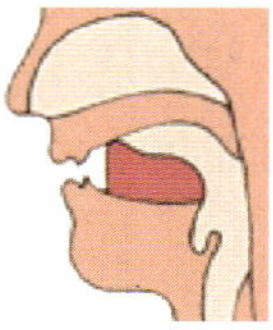	清辅音	舌尖向上卷起，抵在上齿龈后部；双唇收圆，稍向前突出，气流冲破舌尖和齿龈之间的阻碍，发出 /t/ 后立即发 /r/；不振动声带，发出此音
/dr/	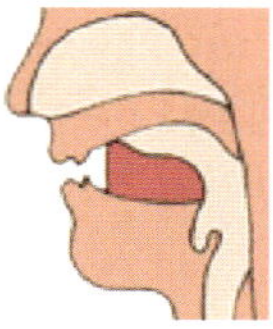	浊辅音	舌尖向上卷起，抵在上齿龈后部；双唇收圆，稍向前突出，气流冲破舌尖和齿龈之间的阻碍，发出 /d/ 后立即发 /r/；振动声带，发出此音

鼻音发音规则

/m/	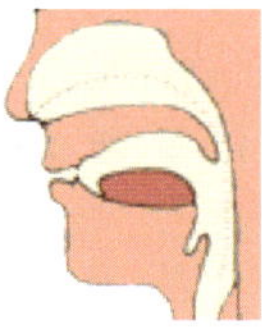	浊辅音	双唇闭拢，舌部平放；气流由鼻腔流出；振动声带，发出此音
/n/	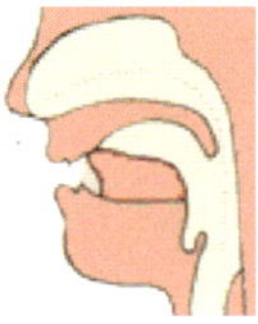	浊辅音	舌尖轻触上齿龈，舌叶轻碰硬腭，嘴微张；气流由鼻腔流出；振动声带，发出此音
/ŋ/	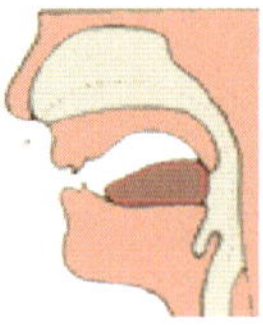	浊辅音	舌后部紧贴软腭，嘴微张；气流由鼻腔流出；振动声带，发出此音

半元音发音规则

/w/	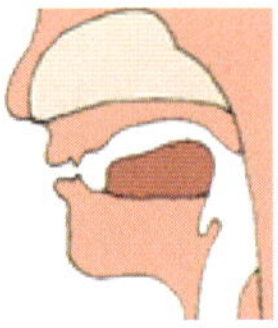	浊辅音	舌后部向软腭抬起，舌位高，双唇呈圆形；气流从抬起的后舌与软腭之间的间隙通过，产生摩擦；振动声带，发出此音
/j/	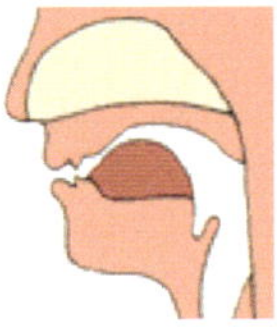	浊辅音	舌前部向硬腭抬起，舌位高，双唇向两旁伸展成扁平状；气流从抬起的舌身与硬腭之间通过，产生摩擦；振动声带，发出此音

Appendix 1

舌侧音发音规则

/1/	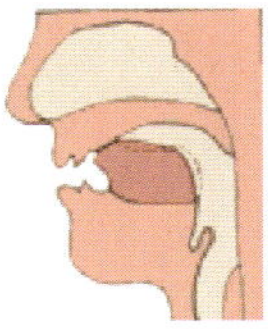	浊辅音	舌尖抵住上齿龈，舌身前高后低，气流从舌头两边流出；振动声带，发出此音。清晰 /1/ 发音时，舌前向硬腭抬起，舌尖抵住上齿龈，舌身平直，气流从舌的一侧或两侧逸出。含糊 /1/ 发音时，舌尖抵上齿龈，舌面形成凹槽，舌向上抬，气流从舌的一侧或两侧逸出

Appendix 2

Stress

重读

英语的重音或重读是指在单词或短语中加强发音的部分。重读音节发音较重，大多数情况下音调更高、语速较慢、音长拉长、响度更响、音质更加清晰。正确地重读可以使说话者在使用英语进行口语表达时更加自然和舒适。

一、单词的重读

英语中的单音节词只有一个音节，该音节为天然的重读音节。

英语中两个或两个以上音节的单词中，通常至少会有一个音节需要重读，作为主重读音节，该音节前会标记重音符号“ˈ”；除主重读音节外，部分多音节词还需要在某个音节上次重读，次重读音节前会标记次重音符号“ˌ”。例如：

mother /ˈmʌðə(r)/

machine /məˈʃiːn/

impossible /ɪmˈpɒsəbl/

international /ˌɪntəˈnæʃnəl/

strawberry /ˈstrɔːbəri/

二、短语的重读

英语中的短语通常由多个单词组合而成。短语的重读通常落在表示该组短语核心意义的中心词的重读音节上。例如：

be <u>good</u> at

come <u>out</u>

full moon

三、句子的重读

英语句子中，并不是每一个单词都需要重读。句子中需要重读的单词的重读音节则构成句子的重音。

句子重音可以分为语法重音和逻辑重音两种。

1. 语法重音

简单来说，语法重音就是英语句子中按照英语语法结构的特点需要重读的音，通常是句子中的名词、动词、形容词、副词、数词等实词。而句子中的介词、连词、冠词、人称代词、助动词等则通常不需要重读。如果整句都没有特别需要强调的地方，那么这句话的重音一般落在该句的最后一个实词上。例如：

He will tell you.

It's beautiful!

He is a good boy.

2. 逻辑重音

事实上，英语句子中的任何一个单词都可以根据说话者想要表达的意图，以重读的方式进行突出强调，这种重读就是逻辑重音，主要是帮助说话者表达当时的心情或抒发情绪。例如：

Tom likes to play football with his classmates.

这个句子可以通过重读不同的单词来表达不同的强调对象。

◇ Tom likes to play football with his classmates.（是汤姆而不是其他人）

◇ Tom likes to play football with his classmates.（是喜欢而不是其他情绪）

◇ Tom likes to play football with his classmates.（是踢足球而不是做其他事）

◇ Tom likes to play football with his classmates.（是和同学而不是和其他人）

Appendix 3

Liaison

连读

英语句子在口语表达时，并不会将每一个单词都进行清晰的停顿，这样会造成单词和单词的孤立，影响句子的整体流畅性。通常同属一个意群且相邻的两个词在意义上有密切关系，那么说话者可以按照一定规则将一个单词的词尾和后一个单词的开头相连形成一个音节，并连贯地说出，构成连读。

连读所构成的音节一般都不重读，顺其自然地一带而过即可。

常见的连读形式有以下几种：

1. 辅音+元音

当前一个单词的结尾发音为辅音，后一个词的开头发音为元音时，那么这一组辅音与元音可以组成一个音节进行连读。例如：

Good afternoon.

Not at all.

2. r/re+元音

当前一个单词是以-r或者-re结尾，后一个词的开头发音为元音时，r或re要发出清晰的/r/音，并与后面的元音合成一个音节进行连读。例如：

There is a football under it.

Here are four eggs.

3. 辅音+半元音

当前一个单词的结尾发音为辅音，后一个词的开头发音为半元音/j/和/w/时，那么这一组辅音与半元音可以组成一个音节进行连读。例如：

Thank you.

Could you help me?

4. 元音+（半元音）+元音

当前一个单词的结尾发音为元音，后一个词的开头发音也为元音时，这两个元音之间可以增加一个滑音使其连在一起，合成一个音节进行连读。

主要分为以下两种情况：

①前一个单词以元音/iː/、/ɪ/、/eɪ/、/aɪ/、/ɔɪ/结尾时，前后两个元音中间可用很轻的/j/相连。例如：

He is my uncle. /hiː(j)iz maɪ(j)ʌŋkl/

②前一个单词以元音/uː/、/u/、/au/、/əu/结尾时，前后两个元音中间可用很轻的/w/相连。例如：

two others /tuː(w)ʌðəz/

5. 辅音+h

当前一个单词的结尾发音为辅音，后一个词的开头发音为清辅音/h/时，那么前面单词结尾的辅音可直接与后面单词/h/后的元音组成一个音节进行连读，字母h不发音。例如：

give him /gɪvɪm/

let her /letə(r)/

6. 失去爆破

失去爆破，又叫不完全爆破，是指在英语发音时，辅音中的爆破音/p/、/b/、/t/、/d/、/k/、/g/在某些情况下不发生爆破，而仅做出和发爆破音时完全相同的口型，在口腔中形成阻碍，而不将气息送出，只是停顿一下，使得带有不完全爆破音的单词或句子听起来好像爆破音都被吃掉了，从而使前后音节自然流畅地衔接起来。

失去爆破多发生在以下几种情况下：

①爆破音 /p/ 、/b/ 、/t/ 、/d/ 、/k/ 、/g/相邻时，前面一个爆破音不完全爆破。例如：

a(c)tor

ne(ck)tie

bla(ck)board

Si(t) down.

I can'(t) come.

I don'(t) believe he is a ba(d) boy.

②爆破音 /p/ 、/b/ 、/t/ 、/d/ 、/k/ 、/g/在 /tʃ/ 、/dʒ/ 、/m/ 、/n/ 、/θ/、/ð/ 的前面时发不完全爆破音。例如：

pi(c) ture

o (b) ject

kin(d)ness

He is a goo(d) child.

Try on this bla(ck) jacket.

Goo(d) morning.

Goo(d) night.

I don'(t) know.

You may kee(p) the book if you need it.

③爆破音 /t/ 、/d/ 在 /l/ 、/s/ 前发不完全爆破音。例如：

mos(t)ly

frien(d)ly

sa(d)ly

ou(t)side

mi(d)summer

Appendix 4

Intonation

语调

语调是英语语音的重要组成部分，主要指说话时每句话中声调高低抑扬轻重的配制和变化。说话者说出的每句话，都有声音高低的起伏和抑扬顿挫的停顿，并伴随着一定的节奏，这种声音的时高时低、时升时降的变化与语句重音结合在一起就构成了英语语调。

英语语句的完整语义，除了词汇意义之外，还包含语调意义，即说话者用语调所表达的态度或语气。二者结合方能发达出说话者完整的意思。同样的句子，语调不同，意思就会不同，会给听者不同的感受。

英语语调主要有三大类：降调（↘）、升调（↗）和平调（→）。除此之外，有时升调会和降调混合使用。

1. 升调

升调主要用来表示不确定、不完整或说话人礼貌、委婉、轻蔑等情绪。

①用于一般疑问句，表示怀疑和不肯定。

Is he making a kite?↗

②用于选择疑问句或并列陈述句前面的选择部分，表示列举事物。

Do you like beef↗, chicken↗, or fish?↘

For each incomplete sentence, there are four choices marked A↗, B↗, C↗, and D. ↘

③用于陈述句，表示疑问、怀疑、未定、猜测或期待等。

You are angry with me? ↗

④用于祈使句，表示委婉的请求或礼貌。

Excuse me, sir. ↗

⑤用于句首状语的末尾，表示句子不完整，还有后续内容。

A few days later↗, he arrived home.↘

⑥用于反意疑问句的附加问句，表示不确定。

You are a student↘, aren't you?↗

⑦用于特殊疑问句，表示友好或关心。

Where are you from?↗

2. 降调

降调主要用来表示确定或完整的含义，表达说话人决断、肯定、不容置疑等情绪。

①用于陈述句，表示确定。

That street is two miles long. ↘

②用于特殊疑问句，表示内容完整。

What has happened to him? ↘

③用于祈使句，表示命令。

Go back to your seat! ↘

④用于感叹句，表示确定。

What a small world! ↘

⑤用于选择疑问句中“or”之后的部分，表示列举完毕。

Would you like coffee↗ or tea? ↘

⑥用于反意疑问句的前一部分，表示对事物的肯定陈述。

Let's go shopping together↘, shall we?↗

3. 平调

平调为平直调，主要指句子语势平直舒缓，没有明显的高低升降变化。主要用于陈述、说明类的句子，来表达说话人庄重、悲痛、冷淡等感情。